Personality

The psychometric view of personality is well established but little dealt with in most textbooks. *Personality: the Psychometric View* sets out psychometric methods and clearly describes the technicalities of testing and factor analysis. In it, Paul Kline discusses different types of personality tests and examines the main findings from the application of these tests and methods. He further shows their utility in the applied fields of clinical, occupational and educational psychology, as well as drawing out many theoretical implications.

Personality: the Psychometric View is the only text on the psychometric analysis of personality which is written for students, yet also deals with the technical problems in this area, and reviews the work of all the main researchers such as Cattell, Eysenck, Guilford and Jackson.

Personality: the Psychometric View is designed for all students of psychology, education and the social sciences, as well as those in the medical sciences who need to know about personality. Like its companion volume *Intelligence: the Psychometric View*, it will also be useful to more advanced postgraduates who need to use personality tests in their work.

Paul Kline is Professor of Psychometrics at the University of Exeter.

Other books by Paul Kline available from Routledge:

Intelligence: the Psychometric View

The Handbook of Psychological Testing

Psychology Exposed: Or the Emperor's New Clothes

Psychology and Freudian Theory: An Introduction

Fact and Fantasy in Freudian Theory (second edition)

Personality

The psychometric view

Paul Kline

ROUTLEDGE

London and New York

First published 1993
by Routledge
11 New Fetter Lane, London EC4P 4EE

Simultaneously published in the USA and Canada
by Routledge
29 West 35th Street, New York, NY 10001

Typeset in Bembo by Michael Mepham, Frome, Somerset
Printed and bound in Great Britain by
Biddles Ltd, Guildford and King's Lynn

British Library Cataloguing in Publication Data
A catalogue record for this book is available from the British Library.

Library of Congress Cataloging-in-Publication Data
Kline, Paul.
Personality : the psychometric view / Paul Kline.
p. cm.
Includes bibliographical references and index.
1. Personality assessment. 2. Personality tests. 3. Psychometrics
I. Title
BF698.4.K57 1993
155.2'8—dc20 92–38182
CIP

ISBN 0–415–08977–8
0–415–08978–6 (pbk)

Contents

Chapter 1

The meaning of personality

The term personality has many meanings in psychology. Indeed it has been claimed by Hall and Lindzey (1957) that there are as many definitions as there are theorists. This is a serious matter for the scientific and systematic study of personality since, clearly, definitions of terms affect the content and method of what is studied. For example, the subject matter of papers in psychoanalysis, especially modern research, bears almost no relationship to that of situationalists such as Mischel (1968, 1977) or social learning theorists, typified by Bandura (Bandura and Walters, 1963). In this first chapter, therefore, it will be necessary to see to what extent there is common ground within these different approaches to personality and to delineate the trait account which underlies the psychometric view.

Different theories of personality

It is not possible, or necessary, to describe in detail all personality theories. Here I shall set out the main points of some of the most influential theories and show how these theories have within them different definitions and concepts. All this means, of course, is that unless considerable common ground can be found, any research devoted to one theory will seem useless from the viewpoint of another. That is why it is essential to clarify definitions and concepts.

Psychoanalytic theories

Classical psychoanalysis, as typified by Freud (1939), Jungian theory (Jung, 1940), more modern American psychoanalysis (Fromm, 1965) or the recent French version (Lacan, 1966), has the unconscious, although differently described, as a key concept. Psychoanalytic studies of personality must, difficult as this is, take this into account. This profoundly affects method. Freudians stress the importance of defence mechanisms, such as repression and reaction formation, the Oedipus and castration complex, and the drives of sexuality and aggression. Child development is an important aspect of the theory, especially psychosexual development, and underlying everything is a closed energy model, instantiated in a mind conceptualised as id, ego and superego, forces in fine equilibrium.

Jung's theories also embrace the closed energy model although the descriptions of the mind are different and the aim of therapy and life (analytic psychology is nothing if not bold) is not ego control but individuation, a blend of persona and the wisdom of the collective unconscious, attractive but certainly not attained by Jung and probably unattainable.

For Jung and Freud, personality is seen as resulting from the equilibrium of the mind which is conceptualised even in two such essentially similar theories in concepts which are markedly different. For example, to study the collective unconscious would throw little light on the Oedipus complex. Clearly these concepts and definitions of personality demand quite separate research.

Perhaps even more important is the fact that psychoanalytic theories in general demand a way of looking at the problems of personality which to their adherents seem so natural as to be unnoticed. Thus the mind is seen in terms of depth (the theories are sometimes called depth psychologies). Generally the more deeply seated phenomena are the more important; everything is caused; childhood experiences and fantasies are crucially influential, and self-knowledge, on account of the unconscious, is impossible without analysis, except for the master. Such a psychoanalytic view of personality profoundly affects what appears to be important in the field and thus the research and scholarship which might be undertaken.

This view of personality is in stark contrast to that of Bandura and Walters (1963) whose social learning theory is essentially, as the name suggests, a special application to personality of operant learning theory, as propounded by Skinner (e.g. Skinner, 1953). For these behaviour is the important component of personality. Mental events because they are not public are not worthy of scientific study and, of course, they are not amenable to it. Phobias, for example, are regarded in this theory as learned maladaptive responses. Personality is a set of learned behaviours. This is different indeed from the psychoanalytic conception, of whatever school, of a phobia as arising from deeply buried unconscious conflicts.

The research undertaken by social learning theorists into personality will be concerned with establishing the patterns and conditions of reinforcement which are salient for personality development and change.

These will be entirely different from psychoanalytically based research. What is defined as personality by these two approaches has little in common, although both see parents as important influences on personality.

One aspect of social learning theory which separates it entirely from earlier psychoanalytic ideas must be mentioned briefly here although it will be dealt with in detail later in this chapter. This concerns the scientific method. Most modern personality theories attempt to be scientific in the Popperian sense (Popper, 1959). This means that they are set out such that they may be falsified. This demand, as shall be seen, has undoubtedly affected the development of these theories and this is particularly true of the psychometric approach.

Mischel (1968) originated what has been called situationalism, because he argues that personality traits, far from accounting for personality, are variables of relatively little importance because behaviour is far more determined by the situation in which individuals find themselves. For this reason, it is asserted, the correlations between personality traits and external criteria are usually small. For example, a person may well appear extraverted at a party or football match but will appear introverted, if observed at a funeral or in a large library.

I shall not say more here about situationalism because its influence has affected the modern psychometric account of personality, at least in principle. However, there is no doubt that research driven by situationalism is very different from that emerging from trait psychology.

Situationalism, because it attacked trait psychology and the psychometric approach, is a useful entrance to the subject matter of this book, the psychometric view of personality. However, before I turn to this it is instructive to mention briefly yet another attempt to deny the importance of personality traits. This is attribution theory which has been well summarised by Eiser (1980). Essentially this asserts that traits are in the eyes of the beholder. Traits are attributed to individuals as explanations of their behaviour. They result from the cognitive processes of observers which have to be studied rather than the actual behaviour of those who are observed. The weakness of this position is that it denies the possibility that traits are influential in determining behaviour. Logically both positions could be true. Nevertheless, it illustrates the point, perhaps with even greater clarity than could be done with the other theories, that definitions of personality are intertwined with theoretical viewpoints.

Conclusions from descriptions of personality theories

I have described the essentials of a number of personality theories to demonstrate that the definitions and concepts of personality are dependent on particular theories and viewpoints. Furthermore, theories of personality affect the kind of research and the methods of investigation which are used so that there may be little in common between the results of different approaches to personality. It would be surprising, therefore, if any one theory were all embracing, although psychoanalytic theories do make such claims. Clearly, however, given these problems it would be advantageous if a particular approach to the study of personality could cover much of the ground.

Trait theory of personality

As Kreitler and Kreitler (1990) point out, the everyday conception of personality is in terms of traits. Traits are conceptualised as stable tendencies or characteristics of individuals. Since it is obvious that people differ in terms of traits, it is natural that the psychometric view of personality should be a trait theory, for psychometrics is the study of individual differences. The psychometric view of personality, therefore, arises from the study of individual differences in personality traits.

Personality traits are used, in trait theories, to answer two fundamental questions, those concerning the determinants of behaviour and the structure of personality – how traits are related. Thus to a trait theorist personality is the sum of an individual's traits and these traits explain that person's behaviour. The research questions, therefore, in trait psychology involve the number and nature of personality traits and their relations to behaviour.

The psychometric view of personality, or what might be called the psychometric model of personality, constitutes the answers to these two questions which have been obtained from the psychometric study of personality. It is these answers and the methods from which they were derived which form the core of the present book.

It should not be thought that the psychometric view of personality and the trait view are identical. This is not the case because it is possible to develop a trait view without psychometrics, or only partly based on psychometrics, as was done, for example, by Murray (1938). McDougall (1932), indeed, expounded an important and influential trait theory without tests of any kind. However, as shall be argued throughout this book, the psychometric view of personality can offer a greatly improved version of the trait model, because it is based upon sound measurement.

The psychometric model of personality

Definition of personality

In the psychometric model, personality is defined as the sum of an individual's traits which determine all behaviour. Thus, as shall be seen later in this book, it is possible to write specification equations for a variety of behaviours in terms of traits. In some cases good predictions can be made from them. Before explicating this model in the remainder of this book, it is necessary to point out some of its advantages compared with other models or views of personality.

The psychometric model and scientific method

Throughout this book it is assumed that the best method to obtain valuable knowledge about human personality is through the scientific method. This is not an article of faith but is derived from the fact that in the natural sciences the application of the scientific method has led to an enormous increase in understanding. However, the subject matter of psychology differs so considerably from that of the natural sciences that it is arguable that the scientific method is not well suited to it. Indeed I have demonstrated (Kline, 1988) that in many branches of psychology the scientific method, at least as conceived by its practitioners, manifestly fails. However, in the field of personality, the scientific method, as represented by psychometrics, seems able to make some progress.

Essence of the scientific method

As was discussed earlier in this chapter, a critical aspect of the method lies in the formulation of refutable hypotheses. In practice this has demanded that research in the field of psychology has certain characteristics which are set out below.

- —All variables should be quantified. Of course quantification can take various forms and the higher the precision the better.
- —Samples should be large and representative. On account of the heterogeneity of human beings and their enormous numbers sampling is essential in all experimental work. Clearly samples must be adequate if conclusions beyond the experimental results are to be drawn.
- —Statistical analyses should be carried out. It is essential that statistical

analyses be carried out to show to what extent the results could have arisen by sampling error. This is the problem which arises from most clinical studies. However, as will be fully discussed in the relevant sections of this book, many statistical analyses reported in the research literature are so poor as to be misleading. The reverse of this error is also often found, as has been shown by Kline (1988). Here researchers are so determined to produce sound statistical work that they choose problems easy to analyse but of a profound triviality.

— Research designs should be such as to allow proper conclusions to be drawn. This aspect of the scientific method is closely related to the statistical analysis discussed above. However, in many studies of psychotherapy, for example, no control groups who receive a placebo treatment are used. This makes evaluation impossible.

— Hypotheses should be drawn up such that they may be refuted. This is the critical aspect of the scientific method. However, only by ensuring that the four points above are properly executed is it truly possible to refute hypotheses.

Nevertheless, despite its apparent simplicity, a few comments should be made about the principle of refutability. First it means that no scientific knowledge is fixed but is always held true until it is refuted. Furthermore, it should be pointed out that hypotheses cannot be proven, only refuted. An obvious example of this can be seen with the hypothesis that all swans are white. This hypothesis can never be proven no matter how many white swans are observed. It may be held until refuted by observing a black specimen. It should further be noted that a hypothesis need only be logically refutable to be scientific. Thus before the development of space rockets it was quite scientific to hypothesise that the moon consisted of cheese or any other substance since this was, in principle, testable.

Finally there is another, perhaps more fundamental, difficulty associated with the notion of refutability. This concerns its meaning. As Gruenbaum (1984) has argued, careful analysis indicates that the only meaning which can be attached to the claim that some hypothesis is not refutable is that the individual making that claim cannot think how it might be refuted. Nevertheless, despite this problem, as an effective, practical approach to carrying out scientific research the Popperian notion of science as depending upon the formulation of refutable hypotheses is highly valuable.

From this analysis of the scientific model it can be argued that psychometrics and, therefore, the psychometric model is well able to meet the demands of good scientific work. Thus psychometrics is concerned with the development of psychological tests thus ensuring as sound quantification as possible. Similarly psychometrics has always placed great emphasis on sampling, research design and statistical analysis, as can be seen, for example, in Nunnally (1978), Cattell (1978) and Kline (1992a). This is one important advantage of the psychometric model of personality compared with other approaches. Thus it is notoriously difficult to put psychoanalytic theory to a rigorous scientific test, although by no means impossible (Kline, 1981).

There is a further advantage inherent in the psychometric view of personality. This is simply that it is virtually all embracing. It claims that all behaviour can be understood in terms of traits. If at present this seems to be impossible, this is only because of shortcomings in measurement and in the mathematical conceptualisation of the problems of personality, at least as argued by Cattell (1981).

Before concluding this chapter a little more needs to be said about traits. In the English language there is a huge number of trait terms. Traits which seem to be concerned with problem solving, such as intelligence, a pervasive trait, are usually conceptualised as ability traits. These have been shown (Cattell, 1957) to be separate from personality traits in the sense that the correlations between traits in these different fields are generally low and non-significant. However, there is a distinction to be drawn among personality traits themselves. This is between temperamental and dynamic traits. The former account for how we do what we do, the latter for why we do it. To exemplify the distinction, extraversion is a temperamental trait. Extraverted individuals can be easily spotted. As they do things they make a lot of noise and expend a great deal of energy. If other people are about they talk and joke with them. Dynamic traits, on the other hand, are drives. Fear can be a powerful drive as is sex or hunger.

A distinction can also be made between states or moods and traits. Traits are relatively constant, enduring characteristics of an individual, whereas states are transient. Anxiety is particularly interesting in this respect because there is clearly trait and state anxiety. Trait anxiety is the general level of anxiety which each individual has, if nothing particularly arousing has occurred. State anxiety reflects the anxiety provoked by some event or thought. Visits to the dentist, examinations and unusual situations are all likely to arouse state anxiety.

In the relevant chapters of this book, these distinctions will be fully discussed and the basis for them will be examined together with their implications for the psychometric view of personality. Here it is sufficient to note that they exist.

Conclusions

In this chapter I have described briefly a number of different theories or views of personality to demonstrate what is inevitably the case that definitions and concepts used in the study of personality depend upon the theory involved. This is important because there are many different theories of personality, with relatively little overlap. In this context the psychometric model of personality was described and its relation to the more general trait model was explicated.

It was shown further that the psychometric model of personality was consonant with the scientific method as applied to the study of personality with its demand on precise quantification and the clear formulation of testable hypotheses. It was also shown that the psychometric model of personality is comprehensive in its coverage since it claims to be able to account for all behaviour in terms of traits.

The remainder of this book will be concerned with a description and scrutiny of the psychometric view of personality, an examination of its application in various applied fields of psychology and finally of its contribution to psychological theory and knowledge. In Chapter 2 the measurement of personality is discussed.

Chapter 2

Measurement of personality

Personality tests

Since the early days of psychology, there have been attempts to measure personality, with a variety of different kinds of tests. As a result of this considerable research effort, in the modern study of personality there are now three kinds of psychological test in general use: personality questionnaires or inventories (these terms are absolutely interchangeable); projective tests; and objective tests.

Before describing these different types of personality tests, a few more general points about psychological measurement need to be made, thus enabling a fine examination of personality measurement.

The characteristics of good psychological tests

Psychometrics is the study of individual differences by means of psychological tests. Psychometricians, as specialists in measurement, attempt to produce tests with certain key features and these are set out below. They are the essentials of precise measurement and are thus critical for the proper application of the scientific method.

All good tests should be highly reliable, valid, discriminating and have good norms. The meaning of these terms will now be discussed. To do this, however, a number of concepts require some explanation.

Universe of items Any set of items in a test is assumed to be a random sample from a universe of relevant items. This universe is, of course, notional and infinite. The better the sample of items the better the test. The score on a psychological test is known as the obtained or the fallible score. This is to be distinguished from the true score. Any fallible score consists of true score + error.

True score The true score consists of the score of a subject on the universe of items. This is, therefore, a notional score. However, as shall be seen, it can be estimated from the obtained or fallible score provided that the reliability of the test is known. Since the square root of the reliability of a test (its homogeneity and its dependability over time, but see below) is an estimate of the correlation of the test with the true score, it can be seen that the higher the reliability the less the error of the test and the more closely the obtained scores approximate the true scores.

All this is part of classical test theory and is expounded with brilliant clarity in Nunnally (1978).

Reliability

Reliability has two meanings which will be scrutinised separately. One concerns the internal consistency of a test, the other its stability over time – known as test-retest reliability.

Internal consistency reliability Any measure, not simply a psychoogical test, should be internally consistent. If different parts of it are measuring different variables it is hard to see how it could be a good test. For this reason internal consistency is regarded as a desirable attribute of tests. It should also be pointed out that in psychometric theory (see Nunnally, 1978 or Kline, 1986) it can be shown that reliability is inversely related to error of measurement. The only dissenting voice among leading psychometrists, is that of Cattell (1973) who argues that high internal consistency can lead to the measurement of rather narrow and psychologically trivial variables. His ideal is a test in which all items correlated with the variable which they were supposed to measure but not at all with each other. There is good logic in this argument but in practice it is almost impossible to construct tests of this type. In the view of this writer, high internal consistency reliability is essential but not too high because of the dangers of measuring trivial variables, which undoubtedly occur in social psychology, for example, as has been shown in Kline (1992a).

How reliability is measured must now be discussed. The simplest method is to split the test in half and correlate the two sets of scores – the split-half reliability. However, since a test can be split in many ways this may be inaccurate and in fact Cronbach's alpha (Cronbach, 1951) is the preferred coefficient. This provides an estimate of the correlation of the set of test items with another set of similar items from the same universe of items. The square root of alpha is the estimate of the correlation of the test with the true score, as was pointed out above. This makes it clear why internal consistency reliability is regarded as so important. The higher it is the less error. In fact an alpha of 0.7 is regarded as a minimum figure for an adequate test.

It might be thought that there is some confusion, or even contradiction, in the first claim that tests must be internally consistent since the higher the reliability the less the error, and the argument of Cattell, that internal consistency should not be too high. However, this is not the case. Tests can be made highly consistent by using items which are virtual paraphrases of each other. These are highly reliable, but in terms of classical test theory, they are samples of a universe of items of little psychological interest – items which are semantically similar to each other.

Classical test theory is statistical not psychological, with the result that it is concerned simply with universes of items but is uninterested in the psychological meaning of these universes. If we consider a universe of extraversion items, it becomes obvious that this is broad and that items which are genuinely part of it may not correlate highly with each other. Thus both Cattell and classical test theory are correct and in practice it seems best to aim for tests with alphas beyond 0.7 but to be suspicious, especially in the sphere of personality as distinct from ability, where alphas can be high, of alphas beyond 0.9. This problem of reliable but narrow and specific tests of little psychological interest will be dealt with in more detail in the next chapter on factor analysis, and will occur again later in this chapter under the heading of validity.

Test-retest reliability There is no need of abstruse psychometric theory or recourse to notional true scores, to understand the psychometric demand that the test-retest reliability of tests be high and again 0.7 is a minimum figure for a satisfactory personality test. It is perfectly obvious that if a test is given on two occasions and gives different scores each time that one, at least, must be wrong and that no trust could be placed in either, provided that the subject tested had not changed.

All this is so banal as, perhaps, to appear hardly worth writing. Yet two of the most common forms of assessment, the interview (used in occupational selection) and the essay (used in education), have notoriously poor test-retest reliability (Vernon, 1964), in some cases little better than zero.

Standard error of measurement

As has been argued above, obtained scores from tests are estimates of true scores. The higher the test-retest reliability the closer to the true score are the obtained scores. The standard error of measurement estimates at different levels of probability what the true score of an individual might be.

Formula for the standard error of measurement, $\sigma_{meas} = \sigma_t / \sqrt{1 - r_{tt}}$ where σ_t = the standard deviation of the test and r_{tt} = test-retest reliability.

The standard deviation of a test is the index of the variability of the scores. In a normal bell-shaped distribution of scores 68 per cent of all scores fall between the mean (average) and plus and minus one standard deviation. 95 per cent of all scores fall between the mean and two standard deviations. For example, if a test has a mean of 50 and a standard deviation of 10: 68 per cent of scores fall between 40 and 60 and 95 per cent between 30 and 70.

Importance of the standard error of measurement The standard error of measurement is highly important if test scores are to be used as a basis of judgement about individuals. This standard error is the estimated standard deviation of scores of an individual taking a large number of parallel sets of items. It can thus be used to set confidence limits around a test score. An example will clarify the point and demonstrate its value.

Suppose that we have a personality test score of a subject of 120 and further suppose that the standard error of measurement is 5. Then 68 per cent of that individual's obtained scores would fall between 115 and 125 and 95 per cent would fall between 130 and 110, if she were to be tested again and again. These are the boundaries of the true score for that individual. Given these standard errors it would be ridiculous to select her for a post over another candidate who had scored 116.

Again if we were comparing the scores of one person on a variety of subscales of a test, differences would have to be beyond the error boundaries to be taken seriously.

The implications of these points are obvious. For all practical testing it is essential that the test be highly reliable. A test with poor test-retest reliability is of little value because its scores give a poor indication of the true score.

Factors influencing test reliability I am stressing the importance of reliability because, as shall be seen, many personality tests, especially projective tests, are so unreliable that they can be used only with the greatest caution. Factors which are likely to make tests reliable include objective scoring, where no judgement is required by the scorer and having a large number of items. It can be shown that the more items a test has the more reliable it is, until it becomes so long that boredom and fatigue set in. This is the Spearman-Brown prophecy formula (see Nunnally, 1978 or Kline, 1992a). A twenty-item test can be highly reliable but a reliable test of below ten items is probably too specific to be useful.

One further point highly relevant to the study of personality needs to be made. Some variables such as moods and states fluctuate quite considerably. Thus the test-retest reliability of measures of fear or anger is likely to be low. While it is true that a measure of anger given on two occasions might have a low correlation, this is not necessarily on account of low reliability. This is because the status of individuals on the variable has changed. A good test ought to register differences. Reliability is concerned with changes due to error, not to function fluctuation, as it is called by Cattell (1973). The correct way to estimate the test-retest reliability of a variable such as anger would be to arouse the anger in subjects on each occasion of measurement.

However, important though test reliability is, as has been shown, it is so only because it contributes to the validity of tests and this must now be discussed.

Test validity

A test is valid if it measures what it claims to measure. However, with this definition all depends upon how what a test measures may be demonstrated. This difficulty has led to a number of different types of validity and these will now be described. It should be pointed out at this juncture that, unlike reliability, there is no single figure which indicates test validity. Indeed, according to some writers, e.g. Vernon (1964), a test is valid for some particular purpose or with some particular group. Thus a test might be valid in the selection of military personnel but not useful for doctors.

Face validity This refers to the appearance of a test. If it looks valid it has face validity. Unfortunately, with personality tests, there is no necessary connection between face validity and true validity. Indeed, the only demand that tests have some degree of face validity is that without it subjects may not cooperate in the testing. This unquestionably lowers the validity of the test. However, if a test is truly face valid, it may lead to distortion, especially in selection. Candidates for the armed services would be unlikely to admit to physical fears, for example.

Concurrent validity To demonstrate concurrent validity, a test is correlated with another test of the same variable, both tests being administered at the same time. For satisfactory concurrent validity a correlation of at least 0.70 between the two tests would be expected. There are several points to be noted about this type of validity. The first concerns the logic of the procedure. If there is a good benchmark test of the variable, then a high correlation is convincing evidence of validity. However, in the field of personality this is rarely the case and only the measures of extraversion and anxiety in the EPQ (Eysenck and Eysenck, 1975) could be regarded as satisfactory for this purpose. Nevertheless, even here there is a problem. If these scales are so good what is the point of another scale? Only if the new scale has real advantages, for example, it is easier to administer, or much shorter than the benchmark scale, is there a point in trying to develop it. Obviously if scales are not themselves highly valid, a high correlation would not be convincing and a moderate correlation would be difficult to interpret. Hence concurrent validity is not much used on its own. However, as one piece of evidence it can be useful. This is discussed below, under the heading of construct validity.

Predictive validity A test is said to possess predictive validity if it can predict some relevant outcome. For example, if a group of people were given an anxiety test, they could be followed up a few years later and the anxiety scores could be used to predict psychiatric breakdown or treatment for psychiatric or psychological problems. If there were a significant correlation, the test would have predictive validity.

This would be an impressive demonstration of validity as predictive validity always is. However, in the case of personality tests it is difficult to set up a good criterion, with the exception of anxiety, so that, as with concurrent validity, it is little used, except as an aspect of construct validity.

Incremental and differential validity These two types of validity are most frequently found in occupational psychology. Incremental validity can be claimed when a test correlates rather low with the criterion score (success at a job, for example) but zero with other tests in the test battery. Such a test is valuable when the multiple correlation between the test battery and the criterion is computed. This will be further discussed in Chapter 8.

Differential validity occurs when a test correlates differentially with different parts of the criterion score. The most usual example of this is to be found in the prediction of academic achievement. Thus intelligence correlates much the same with degree classes in all faculties while interest tests and tests of extraversion have different correlations with different subjects. Vernon (1950) contains a useful discussion of this point.

Construct validity Because, as has been seen, it is difficult to establish the validity of personality tests by any of the methods which have so far been discussed, construct validity is usually the chosen approach. The concept of construct validity was developed by Cronbach and Meehl (1955). The demonstration of construct validity requires that hypotheses concerning the nature of the test variable (construct) be set up. If all of them, or the majority, are confirmed, then the test may be said to be valid. An example, an anxiety test, will clarify the nature of construct validity. The following hypotheses would be tested:

1 High scorers would be more likely to be receiving psychiatric treatment than low scorers.
2 High scorers would be less likely than low scorers to be in stressful or dangerous occupations.
3 The anxiety test will have positive correlations with other anxiety tests.
4 The anxiety test will correlate zero with personality tests not measuring anxiety.
5 The anxiety test should correlate zero with tests of ability and motivation.

If all these hypotheses were supported it would be difficult to argue that the test was not measuring anxiety. From the nature of the construct of anxiety, these are the results which would be expected. It is to be noted that construct validity involves a pattern of results, a mosaic of findings, and this is the cause of one of the difficulties with the concept. In practice results are not so clear cut that all or none of the hypotheses are confirmed. Thus there is a strong subjective element in the assessment of construct validity. Claims for construct validity must be carefully scrutinised.

Conclusions concerning validity It is clear from this discussion that the validity of a test is a subjective issue which cannot be settled by the production of some clear statistic. With the exception of face-validity, each type of validity bears on the question of whether the test measures what it claims to measure although differential and incremental validity are more concerned with the practical utility of the test. Construct validity is the summation of all the findings.

Validity has been discussed at some length because, as will be apparent throughout this book, the psychometric approach to personality seeks to investigate personality by means of valid tests while many of the other personality theorists use assessment methods and tests of low validity (where they even attempt to measure variables) which renders the work useless.

Discriminatory power

This is the third characteristic of good psychological tests which can be dealt with briefly. One of the aims of a good test is to produce a spread of scores – discriminatory power. This is obviously essential for psychometrics, conceived of as the study of individual differences, and is equally obviously important if we consider the value of a test on which all subjects score the same. Given equal reliability and validity the most discriminating test would be best.

Discriminatory power is measured by Ferguson's delta (Ferguson, 1949) which runs from 1 (maximum discrimination) to 0. A normal distribution has a delta of about 0.9 which is perfectly satisfactory. The maximum value is attained by a rectangular distribution where the same numbers of subjects are found at each score. In practice, of course, such a distribution is almost impossible to obtain.

The reason for discussing discriminatory power is that personality questionnaires and inventories usually have high deltas while other assessment techniques such as the interview or rating scales are poor discriminators. Vernon (1950), for example, showed that raters could hold a maximum of nine categories in their heads while interviewers could do little better than use three categories: average, below average and above average.

Test norms

The fourth characteristic of good psychometric tests is the possession of good norms. Norms are sets of scores from clearly defined samples and the setting up of these norms constitutes test standardisation.

Without norms the psychological significance and meaning of an individual's score on a test is unknown. This is, of course, because, unlike many measures used in the natural sciences, personality tests have no meaningful zero. Thus a score of 20 on an extraversion test, for example, is interpretable if it appears from the norms that such a score is exceeded by only 2 per cent of the population.

There is no need to discuss standardisation in any detail here (see Kline, 1992a for further information). It is sufficient to note that the samples on which the norms are based should be large and representative. If they are not, norms can be misleading, worse indeed than useless. The actual form which norms take varies considerably with different tests. The most commonly used are T scores with means of 50 and standard deviations of 10.

Summary and conclusions

Four essential characteristics of good tests, high reliability, validity and discriminatory power, together with efficient standardisation, have been discussed. In the light of this discussion the different kinds of personality tests will be described and scrutinised. However, before this is done one distinction needs to be made. This concerns the difference between nomothetic and idiographic measurement.

1 Nomothetic tests. These are concerned with variables common to individuals. Tests of extraversion or obsessionality fall into this category.
2 Idiographic tests. These seek to measure aspects of personality unique to individuals. An example of such a test would be one aimed to assess the nature of a subject's unconscious conflicts, which, according to psychoanalytic accounts, would be unique.

In principle any type of personality test could be nomothetic or idiographic although in practice personality questionnaires and objective tests fall into the former category whereas projective tests tend to be idiographic.

TYPES OF PERSONALITY TEST

Personality questionnaire or inventories

As the names suggest, these tests consist of sets of items, which are usually questions or statements relating to thoughts, feelings or behaviour. Subjects are required to respond appropriately to these items. The most common types of item are illustrated below.

The Yes/No item Must you be in plenty of time if you have to catch a train?
Yes/No.

This is a useful form of item, found in the EPQ (Eysenck and Eysenck, 1975), since it is relatively simple to write and is applicable to a wide range of behaviour and feeling. However, this simplicity can be regarded as a problem. Thus Heim (1975) regards such items not as simple but simplistic (thus insulting the intelligence of subjects and creating a poor attitude to taking such tests) and certainly it is difficult to catch the full subtlety of human behaviour with such items.

There is a variation on this item in which there is a third category for subjects to use if they are uncertain. However, this category may be too attractive for some subjects, although it is not highly informative, with the result that the questionnaire will not be as accurate for them as it should be. Since there is a substantial correlation (Bendig, 1959) between these two forms, however, it becomes simply a matter of preference which is chosen.

The True/False item I regularly feel sick before exams.
True/False.

This is an item form (used in the MMPI, Hathaway and McKinley, 1951) highly similar to that already discussed. These items usually consist of statements in the first person to which subjects must respond.

The Like/Dislike item Baked beans.
Like/Dislike.

This type of item consists or words or phrases to which subjects have to indicate like or dislike. Clearly all depends on the choice of words and this itself reflects the theory underlying the variables measured. This is not a common form of item but it is used in the DPI by Grygier (1975). This test is derived from psychoanalytic theory and thus contains items of food (oral fixation) and phallic symbols (phallic fixation), just for example.

Items with rating scales People should be more self-controlled.
Strongly agree/Agree/Uncertain/Disagree/Strongly disagree.

These items consist of statements to which rating scales, 5, 7 or 9 categories, are appended. Depending on wording different scales can be used, for example, always to never. In the field of personality Comrey (1970) is the keenest proponent of this type of item because the rating scales allow more precise correlations between items, as is discussed in Chapter 3. In addition, these items are not so obviously simplistic. However, there are two difficulties with these scales. Some subjects tend to avoid the extremes while others use them frequently. Furthermore, there are bound to be differences among subjects in how they interpret the meanings of the scale terms. Finally it should be pointed out that some attitude tests are of this type and are known as Likert scales (Likert, 1932).

Various trichotomous forms These are variants of the Yes/No items which have been discussed. Sometimes, for the sake of good sense, the following forms may be used: generally, sometimes, never; true, uncertain, false; agree, uncertain, disagree.

Forced-choice items These involve competing phrases of which subjects have to choose one. An example item: When I'm feeling really tired I like to: *(a) relax in a hot bath; (b) watch the TV; (c) work out in the gym.* The number of choices can vary from 2 to 5 or even more. These items can be irritating if subjects feel that they hate all possibilities.

Edwards (1959) was a powerful advocate for forced-choice items. He matched the pairs for social desirability in an attempt to eliminate the tendency to endorse items according to how socially desirable it was so to do. This response set will be discussed later in this chapter.

Ipsative scores With forced-choice items in which each choice receives a score on a different scale, resulting scale scores (known as ipsative scores) are negatively intercorrelated. Furthermore, they relate to the relative rank of each scale for each individual taking the test. This means that strict comparison between individuals is not meaningful and norms should not be used. Furthermore, because the scales are artefactually correlated, correlational analyses are impossible to interpret. This rules these tests out for factor analysis (see Chapter 3).

Of course not all forced-choice items are ipsative. If a subject scores 0, 1 or 2 on the same scale depending on her response, the items are entirely suitable for further statistical analyses and comparison with other scores.

In brief, this means that tests with ipsative scores are only suited to discussion with the individual who completed the test and are not useful in the psychometric study of personality.

Although there are other types of item used in personality inventories, the types discussed above embrace the vast proportion of items ever found in tests. From this discussion, the nature of personality questionnaires is clear. I shall now turn to a brief discussion of their advantages and problems.

Problems with personality questionnaires

There are certain problems with the use of personality questionnaires which can be discussed briefly because, in general, careful test construction, which will be examined later in this chapter, can overcome them. Frequently mentioned as difficulties are response sets which determine subjects' answers to items and thus lower the validity of the test. The main response sets are discussed below.

Acquiescence This is the tendency to agree with responses, regardless of their content. Vague items tend to produce this response. One method of dealing with it is to have half the items keyed 'No', thus ensuring that acquiescent individuals are not confused with high scorers on the test. Actually, in test construction items which attract acquiescent responses can be eliminated.

Social desirability This has already been mentioned in connection with forced-choice items. It is the tendency discussed by Edwards (1959), to endorse items on account of their social desirability. Thus he found a high correlation between rate of endorsing an item and judgements of social desirability. That is why he used forced-choice items balanced for this variable. Unfortunately, however, it has been shown that the inevitable small remaining differences in social desirability between the components of forced-choice items become magnified in this context, thus negating the point of the procedure (Corah *et al.*, 1958). Again, it must be said that social desirability can be largely eliminated in careful test construction and validation.

The tendency to endorse extremes Some subjects tend to endorse extremes, when rating scale items are used. This is difficult to avoid but again careful item writing and test construction can minimise the effects as Guilford (1959) has argued.

Conclusions

It can be concluded that these response sets can be largely nullified by careful item writing and even more important by careful test construction and validation as will be discussed later in this chapter.

The other main difficulty with personality questionnaires concerns the ease with which subjects can deliberately distort their results, simply because it is usually easy to see the point of questionnaire items. This is a serious defect if questionnaires are used in a selection procedure. One way to obviate the problem is to include a lie scale consisting of items on which it is easy to detect distorters. The results of subjects who score beyond a certain point on such a scale are ignored. Typical lie scale items are: I have never told a lie; I always keep promises; I always hand in any money which I find.

Another method which seems to work well, as judged by reduction of lie scale scores, is to announce that cheating can easily be detected. Of course, in selection, to be branded a cheat is a considerable threat.

In brief, it can be seen that deliberate distortion can be reduced but, obviously, a test which was not so open is certainly to be preferred in selection.

The advantages of personality inventories

The strength of personality questionnaires is that it is easy by virtue of methods of test construction to make them reliable, at least to determine their validity, to make them discriminating and to establish good norms. Thus the best personality questionnaires do possess the characteristics of good test, discussed earlier in this chapter.

In addition, personality questionnaires are simple to administer and score, especially if presented on a computer as is easily possible, and can be given to large numbers of subjects at once. This makes them well suited to applied psychology.

Since it is clear that many of the advantages of questionnaires come about from methods of test construction these must be briefly described.

The construction of personality questionnaires

I shall not describe in detail how personality questionnaires are constructed because that would not be relevant to this chapter. In any case this can be found in Kline (1986, 1992a). Here I shall delineate enough of the methods for readers to understand how personality questionnaires can be made reliable, discriminating and valid.

Item analysis in test construction The basis of test construction is to administer items to samples of the population for whom the test is intended and thus select items which have been shown to be efficient. In item analysis, efficiency is judged against two criteria.

1 Items are selected if they are discriminating. The measure of this is that not more than 80 per cent or less than 20 per cent put the keyed response. Why this should be is obvious if we consider an item to which all subjects had given the same response. Such an item gives no information concerning individual differences.
2 Items are selected if they correlate beyond 0.3 with the total score. This criterion ensures that all items are measuring the same variable which is essential for a good test whose items are assumed to be from the same universe of items. The higher the items correlate with the total score the higher the internal consistency reliability.

Tests whose items meet these criteria are bound to be discriminating, reliable and usually univariate, measuring one variable. This is important since if tests measure two variables, as sometimes occurs, apparently identical scores from two subjects may be psychologically different. Thus a score of 10 might consist of 5 and 5 on the variables in the one case and 9 and 1 in the other. It should be noted that tests constructed by item analysis, even if reliable and discriminating, still require validation, i.e. it is necessary to demonstrate what the variable which the test measures actually is.

Factor analysis in test construction This is highly similar to item analysis and in most cases gives similar results. Thus items selected by one method would also be selected by the other. Factor analysis, which lies at the heart of psychometrics and is not simply used in test construction, is fully discussed and explicated in Chapter 3.

Factor analysis is a statistical procedure which seeks to account for the correlations between variables with as few dimensions as possible. Thus it is ideally suited to test construction since the aim of the test constructor is to produce a set of items whose correlations are accounted for by one variable – the one the test is supposed to measure.

Thus in factor analytic test construction the items are given to a sample of subjects and factored. All items which load (i.e. correlate with) the main factor or factors, if more than one scale is being constructed, are selected for the test. The other criterion of items being discriminating is also used. Thus discriminating items which correlate with their requisite factors are selected. Again, what the factor is, has to be demonstrated in studies of validity.

The advantage of factor analysis over item analysis in test construction is that it is able to select items which are truly univariate or unifactorial. If a test were made up of items measuring two correlated factors item analysis could produce a mixed test. In general, however, as has been stated, the results of both methods yield similar results. Factor analysis, however, demands larger samples and has certain technical difficulties, which are often ignored and result in flawed tests, in the hands of poor test constructors. All these problems will be discussed in Chapter 3.

There is a different method of test construction – the criterion-keyed method – which was used for the MMPI, the most widely used personality test in the world (Eysenck, 1989). In criterion-keyed test construction, a pool of items is administered to different groups and items are selected if they can discriminate one group from the others. Thus in the case of the MMPI, items went into the test if they could discriminate among nine clinical groups and controls. An item which could discriminate manics went into the manic scale, one which discriminated homosexuals into the homosexual scale and so on. Indeed, from the original MMPI item pool more than 200 such scales have been developed by using it with other groups (Dahlstrom and Walsh, 1960).

There are difficulties with this method of test construction which render it far from ideal. The main problem lies in the fact that groups may differ on more than one variable so that a criterion-keyed scale is not necessarily univariate and may measure a mixture of variables. Consequently that a scale will discriminate among groups gives no precise indication of what it measures. Thus criterion-keyed scales are empty of psychological meaning. This makes theorising on the basis of their results of dubious value. Indeed the use of such tests can, for this reason, hinder the development of psychology. Furthermore, if groups are difficult to define, as is the case in the clinical field, criterion-keyed tests may not discriminate as well on subsequent use. Indeed, tests developed by this method are not recommended except for screening purposes, for example in the armed services where it might be necessary to exclude psychotics, and where the only concern is that they are excluded.

Validating the test

By using item and factor analysis to construct personality questionnaires, it has been shown that reliable and homogeneous tests can be produced. However, it is still necessary to validate these tests. The validation of tests has been discussed in the section on validity, and it is sufficient to repeat here, that generally it is usual to demonstrate the construct validity of personality questionnaires.

It is at this point of test validation, however, that many tests are deficient. For example, the PRF (Jackson, 1974) is a superbly constructed test using item analyses in a highly sophisticated fashion and rendering them as efficient as factor analysis. However, the test variables were derived from Murray's (1938) personological theory which has not been validated and no effort was made by Jackson, in the test manual, to show that his scales measured the needs postulated by Murray. Similar flaws can be found in many of the personality tests used in social psychology (Robinson *et al.*, 1991).

Standardising the test

Test standardisation has already been discussed in this chapter. It is a simple matter in principle to collect norms for personality questionnaires since the tests yield clear unequivocal scores. The only problem concerns the time and money required to collect sufficient samples.

Conclusions concerning personality inventories

From this discussion and description of personality inventories it is clear that they can be made reliable, valid, discriminating measures and with good norms. Thus there is every reason to use them as basis for the scientific study of personality. However, I hope that it is also equally clear from the discussion that personality inventories *per se* are not necessarily good tests. Indeed the majority of them are poor, unreliable and not valid, as is clear from a perusal of any of the Mental Measurement Yearbooks (e.g. Buros, 1979) which contain reviews of current psychological tests.

Although some personality inventories have the qualities required of scientific measures and as such for the basis of the psychometric view of personality, there are other kinds of personality test and these must be described.

Projective tests

Projective tests consist usually of ambiguous stimuli which subjects are required to describe. Their responses are then interpreted to provide assessments of personality. One of the most well-known psychological tests whose fame has spread far beyond the boundaries of psychology is the Rorschach test (Rorschach, 1921), a set of ten symmetrical inkblots. A number of points need to be understood before projective testing can be evaluated.

— Projective tests are generally idiographic as distinct from personality questionnaires which are nomothetic. This means that projective tests are concerned with what is unique to individuals and this is often, as Allport (1937) has stressed, far more interesting than what is common, and more salient to understanding people. The fact that they are idiographic has contributed, without doubt, to their popularity among clinicians, whose work involves understanding individuals, and the same applies to many applied psychologists.

— The ambiguity of the stimuli. Stimuli are generally ambiguous and visual. They are ambiguous because the description of a precise photograph of, for example, a bottle of Guinness, would be likely only to provide a response 'a bottle of Guinness' except among the severely psychotic. To recognise these, no test would be required.

The Rorschach test, as has already been mentioned, uses inkblots as the stimuli. The TAT (Murray, 1938), or Thematic Apperception Test, another famous projective measure, portrays human figures, whose expression and even sex are unclear, in ambiguous contexts. Many other projective measures use human beings, for example, the Object Relations Technique (Phillipson, 1955), while those for children sometimes substitute animals, on the grounds that children will identify better with them (see below for the theory of projective testing). Blum's Blacky Pictures (Blum, 1949) is a good example of this.

— Other kinds of projective test stimuli. Not all projective tests make use of ambiguous stimuli. The House Tree Person test (Buck, 1970), as the name suggests, requires the subjects to draw a house, a tree and a person and to answer certain questions about these drawings. All these responses are then interpreted. Sentence completion techniques on the other hand present incomplete sentences to subjects who have to finish them. These endings are then interpreted. As Semeonoff (1977) points out, in his excellent review of projective tests, there are other types involving solid objects and even aural stimuli but these are rare.

— Meaning of projection and the theory of projective testing. In psychoanalytic theory (Freud, 1911) projection is an ego defence mechanism in which unacceptable impulses are projected on to others. For example, racists may see Black people as over-sexed and aggressive. In projective test theory (Semeonoff, 1977) subjects identify with the ambiguous figures or other stimuli and thus project their own feelings and conflicts on to them. Thus if an inkblot is said to show blood, that represents the aggression or the fear of the respondent. Similarly if, in the TAT, a figure is described as terrified this is supposed to represent the subject.

Two points should be noted: that this use of projection is quite different from that of psychoanalysis and the assumption that subjects identify with the main characters of the picture. There is nothing in general psychological theory to suggest that either of these assumptions should be correct and this theoretical weakness of projective testing (as Eysenck, 1959, has argued) needs to be countered by impressive empirical research demonstrating their validity.

— Reliability and validity of projective tests. The reliability and validity of projective tests has been extensively scrutinised by many authors (Eysenck, 1959; Vernon, 1964; Semeonoff, 1977; Kline, 1992a) and there is little disagreement over the results. In general they are of low reliability and validity. The low reliability is attributable to the fact that almost all projective tests are subjectively scored. This gives rise, inevitably, to inter-scorer unreliability and poor reliability if the same scorer scores the test again. All this is bound to lower the validity of the tests.

Eysenck (1959) has argued that the more rigorous the study of the validity of projective tests the worse the results. He described projective tests, indeed, as little more than vehicles for the rich imagination of clinicians. Vernon (1964) showed that while it is claimed that projective tests measure the inner depths of personality (Murstein, 1963) in fact extraneous variables, such as the race of the tester and her sex and their interaction with the race and sex of the subjects, together with what subjects thought the tests were measuring, all affected the results, findings which make it unlikely that deep aspects of the personality are being measured. Indeed it must be concluded that, as normally administered, there is little evidence for the validity of projective tests.

— Normative data. Because of the nature of the responses, it is difficult, but not impossible, to set up norms for projective tests. Exner (1986) has gone a long way towards this for the Rorschach test, but of course this treats the data nomothetically. Even so, there are bound to be responses which do not fit the norms.

Given all these difficulties the question must be answered as to why psychologists persevere with projective tests. First, it must be admitted that, in general, academic psychologists have abandoned them. Clinicians, on the other hand, continue to use them for the following reasons. The experience of administering projective tests is highly interesting. There is a considerable variance in responses among subjects and these responses appear to be psychologically meaningful and are often easy to interpret along psychoanalytic lines. In a sense, they have high face validity. This has to be considered together with the fact that there is a simplistic aspect to personality inventories, as has been argued.

A second reason for not abandoning projective tests stems from the fact that in the hands of skilled users it does appear that some remarkable results have been achieved. One outstanding example, in this writer's opinion (and this line of argument is inevitably subjective), is the work of Carstairs (1957) with the Rorschach in his study of the Rajputs, data which would have been unobtainable from questionnaires. Murray (1938) in his extensive studies of personality was another brilliant exponent. In brief, projective tests can be sources of remarkable data.

Even if this point were granted, however, it must be noted that a test is not a satisfactory scientific instrument if it cannot be used by reasonably intelligent and trained personnel but requires some special gift or intuition. This is certainly the case with projective tests. Thus we are left with a dilemma: projective tests are sources of rich and unique data, yet clearly on all examinations not valid or reliable, except, possibly, in the hands of a few rare practitioners.

Scrutiny of the problems of projective tests, described earlier in this section, give some hope that this dilemma may be resolved. Clearly much of the difficulty stems from the unreliability of the scoring procedures. If these could be improved, it is possible that validity would also rise, although it should be noted that reliable scoring is necessary but not sufficient for validity. Work of this kind is already in progress. Thus Holtzman (1981) has developed and researched a new form of the Rorschach, the HIT, which utilises short answer questions to a large number of inkblots. This is psychometrically efficient and seems to work well, although it appears less rich than the original form of the test.

Another approach which has been attempted by Holley (1973) and by Hampson and Kline (1977) is to score projective tests objectively. This involves essentially a content analysis of the responses; one for the presence, zero for the absence of a variable. An example will clarify the scoring scheme. If a picture is described by one subject as having a rose in it, rose is a variable and it scores one. All other subjects who put this score one. Subjects who do not mention it score zero. In this way it is possible to score most projective tests. The resulting matrix of ones and zeros can be subjected to various forms of statistical analysis. Holley (1973) favours G analysis which involves a factor analysis of the correlations between subjects rather than variables, thus clustering groups of subjects together. Holley (1973) showed excellent discrimination with the Rorschach, by this method, between depressives and schizophrenics. Hampson and Kline (1977) also found that it would discriminate between various categories of criminals, with the HTP test (Buck, 1970). However, there are various technical problems with G analysis which are fully discussed in Kline (1992a) which render its use more complex than the essence of the method described here. Nevertheless it is a viable procedure for projective test analysis although it turns them into nomothetic measures. In summary, this is a possible method of combining the richness of projective tests with the psychometric efficiency required of good testing.

Conclusions concerning projective tests

From this discussion it can be concluded that projective tests are not satisfactory for the scientific study of personality, being neither reliable nor valid, when administered according to their manuals. Objective scoring schemes and methods of analysis, of which G analysis is only one example, can certainly improve their psychometric efficiency but more research is needed to ensure that by so doing, the unique richness of their data, which is the reason for attempting to increase their efficiency, is not lost.

Objective tests

I shall now examine, rather more briefly, the third category of personality tests – objective tests, defined by Cattell (1957), their main protagonist, as tests which can be objectively scored and whose purpose cannot be guessed by subjects.

In principle, any task which can be objectively scored and whose purpose is impenetrable to subjects can be used as an objective test, given also that there is variance in scores. However, this would lead to a virtual infinity of tests so that in practice it is necessary in the development of objective personality tests to draw on some rationale for the test from experimental or clinical psychology. For example, it was noted in psychoanalysis that delay in free association was evidence of the subject matter touching upon emotional problems or conflicts. Jung (1910), indeed, developed a test on this basis. Thus reaction times to words could be used as an objective personality test. Cattell and Kline (1977) contains a full discussion of principles of objective test construction.

Several points should be noted about this description of objective tests. First it is clear that implicit in it is Cattell's concept of personality as the totality of behaviour which involves understanding the determining factors. Secondly it is obvious that all such objective tests require validation. Since, by definition, what they measure cannot be guessed, it is essential that they have clear evidence of validity.

Examples of objective tests

Cattell and Warburton (1967) contains a description of more than 800 objective personality and motivation tests from which more than 2,000 personality variables have been derived. Most of these are still only at the experimental stage and have relatively little evidence for validity. Clearly, in a chapter of this length, it would be impossible to illustrate even a small proportion of them. Instead I shall simply give a few examples of objective tests to indicate their range and scope.

1 The Fidgetometer. This is a chair with electrical contacts in the seat and arms. This measures movements and is almost always undetected by subjects. Even if subjects knew that they were being measured, it is hard to fake. Is it better to be still or move a lot?
2 The Slow Line drawing test. Subjects are required to draw a line as slowly as possible. Scores derived from this are the length of line and whether subjects cheated or not by lifting their pencils above the paper or stopped drawing.
3 Book titles. Subjects have to choose their preferred book titles. Selection of socially acceptable rather than *risqué* titles is claimed to load on a measure of assertiveness (Hundleby, 1973). The following tests also load this factor.
4 Faster speed of tapping.
5 Faster speed of reading when asked to read at one's usual rate.
6 Greater preference for sophisticated activities.

Anxiety is measured by a number of objective tests, although the validity of these measures is not as high as that of questionnaires.

7 Greater number of admissions of minor wrongdoings or frailties. It should be noted that this is a questionnaire measure. However, it is an objective test because no assumptions are made concerning the truth or falsity of the responses. The measure is simply the number admitted to.
8 Greater acquiescence in answering questionnaires. Note here how what in questionnaires is regarded as an annoying response set in objective tests is used as a measure in its own right.
9 Addition under distraction. Scores on a simple arithmetic test are obtained. Later in the test battery the same additions are presented with jokes written on the sheet. Differences in score and time to complete the additions are noted.

These tests give some idea of the nature of objective tests but a few more general points can be made. Some objective tests are physiological. For example, pupil dilation in the startle response (to a gun shot) is listed in Cattell and Warburton (1967). All projective tests, if they are scored objectively, are forms of objective test, and, as such, certain scores from the Rorschach are listed in the Compendium (Cattell and Warburton, 1967). Questionnaires can be objective tests if responses of a certain kind, e.g. the number of 'uncertain' or extreme responses, are counted regardless of item content.

Few of these objective personality tests have been published as tests. The two most well-known published batteries of objective tests are the

Objective Analytic Battery (Cattell and Schuerger, 1976) which measures ten personality factors and the MAT (Cattell, Horn and Sweney, 1970), measuring ten motivation factors.

I shall not describe or evaluate these tests here because the findings from them will be discussed in Chapters 4 and 6. However, it should be pointed out at this juncture that there are problems concerning their validity. For example, a study of the MAT by Kline and Cooper (1982) found the scales to be of low reliability and ten factors could not be extracted from the items. Similarly ten factors could not be extracted from the OAB and the factors which were extracted loaded, in some cases, on ability tests (Kline and Cooper, 1984b).

Conclusions

The conclusions to be drawn from this discussion of objective tests are clear. These are highly interesting and ingenious measurement devices but are of virtually unknown validity. This is largely because they have been little used beyond a small group of researchers working with or influenced by Cattell. Most psychologists who are not experts in factor analysis have been unable to penetrate the mysteries of the factor analytic arguments supporting their use and their validity. Furthermore, because they lack face validity, they have no direct appeal to testers. Combined with these problems is the fact that they are not easy tests to administer, compared to questionnaires, for example. Thus applied psychologists would have to have clear evidence of validity and utility before they used them. All this means that there is remarkably little normative data for these tests which further discourages their use. All this is sad for psychometrics because, in principle, objective tests have many advantages over the other kinds of personality tests.

COMPARISON OF THE THREE TYPES OF PERSONALITY TESTS

Personality questionnaires are simple to administer and score and have the advantage that they are group administrable. In addition it is possible to make them highly reliable, and to set up good norms. The best of them have also been shown to be valid. This has meant that questionnaires are widely used in the scientific study of personality and, above all, in applied psychology.

On the other hand there is no doubt that personality questionnaires are simplistic and it seems naïve to think that personality can be fully conceptualised in terms of five variables (as are usually derived from questionnaires). On a purely practical point, personality questionnaires are far too obvious and are easily distorted, which is a severe disadvantage as regards their use in selection.

Projective tests, in contrast, capture much of the richness of personality but do so at the expense of reliability and validity, except perhaps in the hands of gifted or intuitive testers. Attempts to score projective tests objectively have been made and deserve further research. However, until the validity of such objective scoring schemes is established it is difficult to use projective tests for substantive investigations of personality.

The same applies to objective tests. For these a great research programme is required to discover what the huge array of objective tests measure. This is worth doing because objective tests are difficult to fake, overcome problems of response sets and are likely to be applicable cross-culturally (certainly compared with many questionnaires). Their objective scoring should ensure high reliability. Thus, in many respects, objective tests are an ideal form of personality test. However, at present, none is able to be used for substantive research.

Having described and evaluated the different types of personality test, upon whose scores the psychometric view of personality is based, in the next chapter I shall describe factor analysis and its application in personality measurement. For it is through factor analysis that the results of personality testing have been made useful both for personality theory and for applied clinical, occupational and educational psychology, as is discussed in Chapters 8 and 9.

Chapter 3

Factor analysis in the study of personality

Factor analysis is a statistical technique central to the psychometrics of personality. Not only have the best personality questionnaires been developed through factor analysis, but even more significantly, factor analysis has been used to determine the most important variables in the field. This, as was discussed in the opening chapter, is vital since there is little agreement among personality theorists.

In this chapter my aim is not to explicate the algebra or computation of factor analysis, of which excellent accounts may be found in Harman (1976) or Cattell (1978) and clear explanations in Child (1991) or Kline (1992a). Rather it is to enable readers to understand the logic of factor analysis and to appreciate the problems which it can solve. In addition, I shall set out the rules for technically adequate factor analyses because with the ease of access of high speed computing in the social sciences, factor analysis is used by researchers with little understanding of its underlying mathematics, with the result that many reported factor analyses are misleading. As shall be seen, this has been a considerable cause of error in the psychometrics of personality.

Definition of terms

First I shall define the terms used in factor analysis. I shall begin with basic statistical definitions since if these are not clear, the rest becomes hopelessly muddled.

Variable

Any characteristic on which individuals, or one individual, over time can vary is a variable. In the field of personality, anxiety or anger are variables.

Variance

This is the variation in scores on a variable of a sample or population. Sample and population must be distinguished. If we are studying anxiety level among twenty-one- year-old males in Great Britain, the population consists of all such individuals. In most research we are forced to use samples of populations and it is essential that samples are representative and sufficiently large to reduce statistical error. As shall be seen, sampling is critical in factor analysis.

Correlation

The correlation coefficient r indicates the degree of agreement between two sets of scores. This correlation is positive if high scores on one variable are associated with high scores on the other. It is negative if high scores on one variable are associated with low scores on the other. The correlation coefficient runs from +1 (perfect agreement) to – 1 (complete disagreement), as would be the case if the order of scores on one variable were a perfect inversion of the scores on the other. A zero correlation indicates that there is no relationship between the two sets of scores.

Since correlations are the basis of most factor analyses in the field of personality it is necessary to say more about them.

Meaning of correlations The square of a correlation coefficient indicates the amount of variance in common between the two sets of scores. For example, a correlation of 0.7 shows that there is 49 per cent of variance in common between the two variables. However, before this figure becomes meaningful the determinants of correlations must be discussed.

One cause of correlations between two variables may be elements common to both. For example, there is a correlation between dogmatism, as measured by Rokeach (1960), and obsessionality. This is because the obsessional personality shares certain characteristics with dogmatism, and some items in measures of these variables are highly similar.

In other instances, however, a cause common to both variables may determine the correlation. There is one outstanding example of this in the field of personality. There is little doubt that there is a correlation between cigarette smoking and lung cancer. Eysenck (1980) however has argued not that smoking causes lung cancer but that the correlation is accounted for by a third factor which causes an individual to smoke and to be liable to lung cancer. This is a perfectly possible interpretation of the correlation and it highlights a critical point about correlations: correlations do not imply causation. Since the war there is a correlation between increases in the mean height of adults and increases in divorce rate. Even sociologists have not argued a causal connection.

Magnitude of correlations The size of the correlation indicates how much variance is in common between two sets of scores, as has been argued. However, this can be distorted by various factors which should always be borne in mind in interpreting correlation coefficients. Since factor analyses are usually based upon correlations, these same distortions can affect factor analyses which is why these must be discussed.

Homogeneity of variance reduces the magnitude of the correlation coefficient. There is a small negative correlation between extraversion and academic success at the university, just for example, presumably because extraverted individuals do not enjoy the lack of activity and concentration required of academic work. However, this small correlation can only be computed within students, i.e. subjects who have been able to do well enough academically to enter the university. If we were to sample the whole range of extraversion (including those so extraverted that they could not attain university standards) and the whole range of academic ability, the correlation would probably be larger. The relationship between homogeneity of variance and the size of correlations can be seen if we consider the case where all subjects had the same score on extraversion. Here the relation of extraversion to any other variable would be bound to be 0.

In many real life studies (as distinct from illustrative examples) samples are restricted in variance, especially ability variance, and this restricts the size of correlations. There are correcting factors which may be applied to estimate the population coefficient from the sample, but in this writer's view, it is better to sample efficiently and ensure a representative correlation coefficient.

The other important distorting factor in correlations is the unreliability of the measures. The lower the reliability the lower the resulting correlation between them. As has been discussed in the previous chapter, any decent test should have a reliability of at least 0.7. However, many personality tests do not reach even this modest criterion and, in consequence, correlations with such scales are lower than they would be if the tests were perfectly reliable. Again there are formulae for correcting the attenuation of correlations due to unreliability but again, in this writer's view, it is better to use reliable tests than to adjust obtained statistics. As

Cronbach (1976) has argued, poor data are always poor data no matter what one does with the figures.

One of the aims of factor analysis is to account mathematically for a set of correlations in terms of a smaller number of variables. Therefore, the more accurately these correlations reflect the population variance and are not artifacts of the homogeneity of the variance in the samples or the unreliability of the tests, then the better the factor analysis will be.

Factor analysis

Factor analysis is a statistical method in which variations in scores on a number of variables are expressed in a smaller number of dimensions. These dimensions are the factors. In the majority of psychometric studies of personality, and indeed in all fields in which psychometrics is used, factor analysis is applied to the correlations between variables. It mathematically accounts for these correlations in terms of a smaller number of factors. The factor analysis computes the correlations of each of the variables with these factors. These are the factor loadings which define the factors.

I shall clarify this general description with a simple example, from the field of personality. Suppose that we had obtained ratings of a large number of subjects on a variety of personality traits, e.g. talkativeness, sociability, noisiness, trepidation, pessimism, tension and so on, and computed the correlations between them. If we had ratings on about 100 variables it would be impossible to work out in one's head any pattern of correlations. Factor analysis is an ideal analytic technique because it attempts to give a mathematical account of the matrix of intercorrelations, with a smaller number of variables than the original set (reducing ranks of the matrix). A matrix is simply a set of numbers arranged in rows and columns, in this case the correlations between the ratings.

In studies of this kind there are often five-factors, the big five referred to in the opening chapter (Digman, 1990), of which two are particularly important. One might well load on the following variables: sociability, noisiness, friendliness, conviviality, energy; the second would load on timidity, fearfulness, feeling sick before big events, poor sleeping, for example.

It has been argued that factors are defined by their loadings: the correlations with the variables. Thus to identify the first factor we have to think what construct in the field of personality fits the description – friendly, noisy, etc. In fact, extraversion as described by both Jung and Eysenck fits well. Similarly the second dimension can be identified as anxiety. In other words, the first two factors, anxiety and extraversion, account for the observed correlations between the variables loading on the factors. As has been mentioned, the factor analysis of personality questionnaires and ratings can usually be reduced to five factors. This means that much of the variance in personality is explicable in terms of five constructs. These would appear to be the most important variables.

In psychometric studies of personality, and the results of these studies will form the bulk of the remaining chapters of this book, it is not sufficient to rely on the factor loadings alone to identify factors. Further experimental work is required to validate the identification.

This schematic example of the factor analysis of personality ratings illustrates clearly how complex data can be simplified by factor analysis. It is impossible for most human beings to hold in their minds the correlations between 100 variables, or even just the 100 variables themselves. For example in attempting to assess what horse might win the Derby there are far too many variables to be considered for most to make a correct choice. What happens is that people select out what they believe are the most important variables and consider those. Factor analysis puts this subjective selection procedure on to an objective statistical basis. In the example from personality, these five factors embrace much of the variance from a huge number of variables. As shall be argued, the statistical basis for selecting variables is superior to the intuitive judgements of personality theorists among whom there is no agreement.

With this preliminary discussion of factor analysis I shall now define some more specific terms and say a little more about factor analysis in general.

Exploratory factor analysis In the illustration of factor analysis in the previous section, it was used to simplify a large set of data, to identify the most important variables. For obvious reasons this is called exploratory analysis. This is much the most common use of factor analysis in the study of personality and in psychometrics generally. However, there are other kinds of analysis.

Confirmatory factor analysis In this method factor analysis is used to confirm hypotheses. Thus, to take the example of the big five, it would be possible to obtain a further set of personality ratings and to investigate whether the data fitted the five-factor hypothesis by using confirmatory factor analysis.

In this technique the factor loadings are hypothesised and the computations involve fitting the target matrix as closely as possible. It is possible to test the fit statistically and modern factor analysts prefer confirmatory analysis because the factors can be confirmed statistically. Nevertheless there are difficulties in its use which will be discussed later in this chapter.

Definition of a factor As Nunnally (1978) points out, strictly a factor is simply a linear combination of variables. These combinations can involve any kind of weightings of the variables – differential, negative, unit, or positive. Factor analytic procedures are methods of calculating these combinations and weights, with the aim of explaining the most variance with the fewest factors, at least in exploratory analysis.

This is the statistical definition. However, most psychologists define a factor as a construct operationally defined by its factor loadings (Royce, 1963).

Factor loadings As has been seen, factor loadings are the correlations of variables with the factors, although in oblique rotations (described below) this is true only of the structure matrix. The importance of factor loadings is tied in with the definition of factors. Thus while everyday definitions of extraversion are bound to vary, the definitions of the extraversion factor are precise: it is defined by loadings on given variables.

There is a further advantage to factor analytically defined concepts compared with normal concepts, over and above their precision. A normal (by which I mean developed through thought or reasoning) concept may be of little value. For example, phlogiston, although ingenious, in fact explains nothing. However, a factor explains variance and, if a large factor, explains a considerable amount. It is, therefore, necessarily a useful concept.

Factor identification It was argued above that factors are identified from their loadings but that identification should be extended to other criteria. There are various reasons for this. Thus in many cases identification from loadings alone is not unequivocal and is not as clear as appears in the examples. Furthermore some authors who are opposed to factor analysis, e.g. Heim (1975), have argued that factors are simply statistical entities which refer to nothing beyond the correlation matrix: an argument which they buttress with the fact that there are many different factor analytic solutions to the same correlation matrix. Consequently, any factor needs external verification.

Certainly, it is good psychometric practice to verify factors experimentally and almost all the factors which will be discussed throughout this book have been thus identified. Heim's point about the multiplicity of factor analytic solutions will be discussed later in this chapter.

Communality This is the proportion of variance of each variable accounted for by the factors. It is important to know how well a factor analysis accounts for the variance in a matrix of correlations. There are several criteria to judge the adequacy of factor analyses of which one is to examine the communality of the variables. To calculate the communality of each variable, the common variance accounted for by the factors, the factor loadings of a variable on each factor are squared and added. Thus for example, if in a three-factor solution, a test of obsessional personality loaded 0.71 on factor 1, 0.02 on factor 2 and 0.10 on factor 3, these factors account for just over 50 per cent of the variance on the test. This is not a particularly good solution since nearly half its variance is unexplained. This is called the unique variance which consists of variance unique to the test and error variance and is of little psychological interest. In another study with different variables and factors the communality could well change. Thus it can be seen that one demonstration of the adequacy of a factor analysis is that the communalities are large. Ideally more than 80 per cent of the variance of each variable should be explained.

Reproducing the correlations

Another measure of the quality of a factor analytic solution is to see how accurately the original correlations between the variables can be reproduced. Simple cross multiplication of the loadings (see Cattell (1978) for a worked example) yields the correlations and the closer to the originals these are the better. The fact that the correlations can be reproduced from a smaller number of factors is another indication of the power of factor analysis in understanding the variance in a correlation matrix.

Eigen values or latent roots A third test of a factor analysis is to see how much variance overall the factor explains. The eigen values or latent roots indicate how much variance each factor accounts for and are calculated by summing the squares of each loading on a factor.

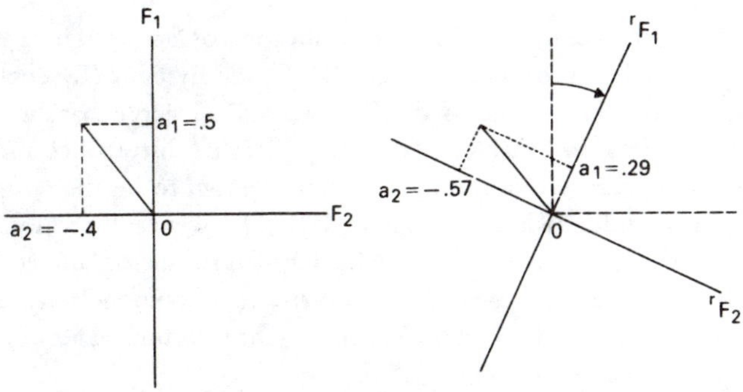

Figure 1 Orthogonal rotation of factor loadings
Source: Adapted from Cattell (1978)

Factor rotation Factors can be conceptualised as axes, as shown in Figure 1.

From this it is clear that factor loadings change, depending upon the position of the axes, although each position is mathematically equivalent. Since factor loadings define factors it is obvious that where rotation should stop is critical to the whole factor analytic procedure. Indeed the fact that there is an infinity of mathematically equivalent factor solutions creates severe problems which must now be scrutinised.

Problems in factor analysis

The essence of the difficulty in factor analysis is simple. On what grounds is one solution from this infinity of possibilities to be chosen? More technically, where does rotation stop? Since there may be no reason, *a priori*, to choose one rotation than another it has led some psychologists, notably Heim (1975), to argue that the method is not valuable.

Indeed, a superficial examination of the results of factor analysis in the field of ability (see Kline, 1991 for a summary), and in the field of personality, would lead one to a similar conclusion for factor analysts appear to propose many different and disparate sets of factors. However, modern factor analysts have overcome all these problems and replicable and meaningful solutions are obtainable. How this can be done and the reasons for these disagreements among different analysts must now be scrutinised. There are both logical and technical difficulties and these will be dealt with separately.

Logical difficulties

One cause of disagreement concerns the identification of factors. There is a clear example of this in the work of Cattell (1957) and Eysenck (Eysenck and Eysenck, 1975), which is discussed in Chapter 4. Both agree that there is a large factor loading on variables relating to psychiatric disturbance and neurotic disorders. Furthermore, they have been shown to be the same factor in empirical studies (Kline and Barrett, 1983). However, for reasons bound up with their own theories, Cattell has labelled the factor 'anxiety' and Eysenck 'neuroticism'. However, this difference of nomenclature is unimportant from the viewpoint of understanding the structure of personality and for its application in applied psychology.

Simple structure

However, as was made clear in the previous section the essential problem of factor analysis – the choice of solution from the infinite possibilities – is more complicated. Thurstone (1947) supplied a logical answer, which still constitutes the principle behind the modern solution to this difficulty.

Each solution may be regarded as a hypothesis to explain the correlation matrix. In the scientific method there is general agreement that if there are competing hypotheses, the simplest is to be preferred – the law of parsimony or Occam's razor. Thurstone, therefore, aimed to rotate the axes to simple structure, this being defined as the most simple position. The essence of rotation to simple structure is to arrive at a solution which maximises the number of zero or near zero loadings. This ensures simple factors each with a few high loadings.

The elegant logic of Thurstone's arguments has received empirical support from the work of Cattell (1978) who has shown that simple structure solutions are replicable and yield meaningful factors in cases where the factors are known. Thus simple structure rotations go a long way to answer the problem of the infinity of solutions.

Unfortunately, as Cattell (1978) has demonstrated, although most of the leading psychometrists agree that simple structure should be the aim of factor analysis, there is little agreement on how simple structure may be obtained. Furthermore, Cattell (Cattell, 1978; Cattell and Kline, 1977) has shown that simple structure cannot be attained unless the factor analysis satisfies certain technical criteria. This is particularly serious because it can also be shown that many published factor analyses are technically flawed. Indeed Cattell (1978) argues that it is these technical errors which have led to the disparity of results. Thus it is now necessary to set out the technical demands of good factor analyses and to discuss the concomitants of the many different types of technical error.

Technical difficulties in factor analysis

Sampling variables

In exploratory factor analyses, as has been discussed, the aim is to map out the field. To do this it is essential that all variables are sampled. For example, if no measures of anxiety were included in a study there could be no anxiety factor. A weakness of many studies is that the selection of variables is arbitrary.

Furthermore a factor requires to be marked by at least three variables which means that one test of a variable is insufficient. Clearly then it is critical that variables be properly sampled in exploratory factor analysis.

Sampling subjects

This is important in factor analysis because if the variance on variables is restricted, factors cannot emerge with any clarity because, as has been argued, correlations become attenuated. This can be important in the field of personality where, for example in normal subjects, abnormal personality factors have low variance.

Numbers of observations and variables

For reasons of matrix algebra it is essential that the number of subjects exceeds the number of variables. If it does not the results are essentially meaningless, as has been shown by Nunnally (1978). However, the number of subjects does affect results as does the ratio of subjects to variables.

Number of subjects

This can be quickly dealt with. The larger the N the better because this reduces the standard errors of the correlations. Where N drops below 100 results should be treated with caution and replication is essential. It is noteworthy in social psychology and health psychology that, where factor analysis is frequently carried out by psychologists who depend entirely on computer programs, Ns fall well below this figure.

Subjects: variables ratio

Here, until recently, there was considerable disagreement among the leading authorities. Nunnally (1978) was the most conservative, claiming a ratio of 10:1 was necessary, while Guilford (1958) was at the other extreme, with a ratio of 2:1.

Barrett and Kline (1981) noted that there was no rationale for any of these ratios other than the experience of the writers. They carried out therefore an empirical examination of this issue in which items from Eysenck's EPQ and Cattell's 16PF Test (both of which will be discussed in some detail in the next chapter) were subjected to factor analysis. With a subjects: variables ratio of 20:1, a factor structure of such clarity emerged that it was used as a baseline with which to compare the results from other smaller samples. It was shown that with a ratio of 2:1 the main factors emerged and that with 3:1 differences from the large sample were trivial.

These findings were essentially confirmed by Arrindel and Ende (1985) who also showed that the ratio of subjects to factors extracted was critical. In conclusion, however, a factor analysis with at least 100 subjects and a subjects:variables ratio of at least 3:1 ought to be sound in respect of statistical error.

Principal components or principal factors

Computing packages all offer the choice of principal components or principal factors and which is preferable must be briefly discussed. First it should be noted that components analysis is not strictly a form of factor analysis because it yields as many factors as variables and explains completely the variance in the particular matrix. Factors on the other hand are hypothetical because they are estimated from the correlation matrix. This makes it more likely, in principle, that they could be generalised to other matrices than could components based on a particular matrix. This is a theoretical point in favour of principal factors.

In computing principal components all the variance in the matrix, including error variance, is explained. Principal factors, by estimating communalities of the variables, attempt to exclude the error variance and Carroll (1983) has argued that this makes principal factors a more accurate procedure. However, Harman (1976) has shown that in large matrices of more than 25 variables there is virtually no difference between the factors.

In this writer's opinion, the distinction is of little practical significance. I have usually computed both methods and the differences are indeed, for the practical purpose of identifying meaningful factors, trivial. Given the faint possibility of inaccuracy in components analysis it would seem sensible to compute principal factors.

Maximum likelihood factor analysis

In recent years this method of initial factoring (based on the work of Joreskog, 1973) before rotation has become popular because programs are now available for the formidable computing involved. This method obtains a set of factors which each in turn explains as much variance as possible in the population matrix, as estimated from the sample correlation matrix. This is, therefore, an inferential statistical method because it seeks to extrapolate from sample to population. Principal components, of course, apply strictly only to the sample matrix.

Maximum likelihood analysis can be used in exploratory factor analysis. If it is, however, rotation is required to give meaning to the factors. However, when communalities and test reliabilities are high the differences between principal components analysis, principal factor analysis and maximum likelihood analysis are small, as was found by Kline and Lapham (1990) in the development of the PPQ.

The claimed advantage of maximum likelihood analysis in exploratory factor analysis arises from the fact that there is a statistical test for the extraction of each factor, whereas other methods of factor analysis are essentially algorithms. However, this statistical test for the number of factors is not always sensitive enough in large matrices to select between various options, thus negating the advantages of its statistical basis.

It may be concluded that for exploratory analyses maximum likelihood methods have little or no advantages over other procedures. However, their main use is in confirmatory analysis and this will be discussed later in this chapter.

Rotating the correct number of factors

Cattell (1978) argues that this is one of the critical issues in reaching simple structure because if too many factors are rotated factors split. If too few factors are rotated a few broad factors are produced, dimensionality being compressed.

Kline and Barrett (1983) examined this problem in considerable detail partly based on their own empirical studies of the problem (Barrett and Kline, 1982). They concluded that there was no one single best method for selecting the number of factors. However, the rotation of factors with eigen values greater than 1, which is the default procedure for many statistical packages, was shown to be unsatisfactory in large matrices considerably over-estimating the number of factors, as Cattell (1978) had argued. Two tests seemed to work well and to be in general agreement: the Scree test (Cattell, 1966) and the Velicer test (Velicer, 1976). However, there is a considerable subjective element in the Scree test which requires some experience and practice with colleagues who can use it. To overcome this Barrett and Kline (1982) developed an automated version, although even in this there is a small subjective element. The Velicer test is quite objective but there is less evidence in support of its validity.

In conclusion it seems best to use both these techniques and if they suggest different numbers of factors both rotations should be made. These methods are guidelines rather than rigid rules.

Orthogonal or oblique rotations

Orthogonal rotations In orthogonal rotations the factor axes are at right angles to each other (as in Figure 1) and are uncorrelated.

Oblique rotations Here the factors are oblique, less than 90 degrees. Oblique factors are correlated, the cosine of the angle between them giving the correlation. It is obvious, if Figure 1 is borne in mind, that as the angle becomes smaller the factors become more similar, until as they take up the same position they become identical.

Thurstone, as has been argued, defined simple structure as a set of factors each with a few high loadings but the majority zero or close to zero. With such a definition it is obvious that oblique rotations should be better able to reach simple structure than orthogonal rotations because their axes can take up any position thus maximising the zero loadings. There is a further argument in favour of oblique factors, namely that in the real world it is unlikely that important determiners of behaviour such as factors would be uncorrelated; points stressed by Cattell (1978) and Kline (1979). Thus almost all factorists of any note support Cattell's position that oblique rotations are essential for obtaining simple structure.

The only exception is Guilford (1959) who claims that while it is true that an oblique factor may be more simple than its orthogonal counterpart, a set of oblique factors is more complex than a set of orthogonal factors because in interpreting them their correlations have to be taken into account. This argument turns on the meaning of simple. However, in the field of personality, as shall be seen, empirical work supports the notion that oblique sets of factors are more replicable and more simple. In any case the argument that orthogonal factors are unlikely in the real world should not be ignored.

There is a further reason why oblique rotations should be preferred. It is possible to factor the correlations between oblique factors. These factors are known as higher-order factors and are more broad than primary factors which load on them. It is often possible to describe large matrices in terms of a few higher-order factors and this is, indeed, a simple solution which is only possible with oblique factors.

In summary, therefore, it must be concluded that oblique rotations are essential if simple structure is to be obtained.

Methods of rotation

Cattell (1973, 1978) reiterates the point with which this writer is in complete agreement that one of the major causes of failure to reach simple structure is poor rotational methods, even when these produce oblique factors. This is a difficult problem because there are now many different oblique rotation programs, although there is some agreement as to the best procedures. I shall summarise the conclusions, although for a more full discussion readers should see Kline (1992a) and Gorsuch (1974) for computational details, because if simple structure has not been obtained, the results of studies, as will be seen in subsequent chapters of this book, must be discounted.

Hakstian (1971) studied a number of oblique rotational procedures and found that the most efficient and best at obtaining simple structure was Direct Oblimin (Jennrich and Sampson, 1966), while the computationally more simple Promax was also good, provided that the factors were not too oblique. If for some reason orthogonal rotation is desired, Varimax is without question the best. There is surprisingly wide agreement concerning the effectiveness of these methods although Cattell (1978) argues that his own technique Maxplane followed by Rotoplot (in which the factors are hand adjusted) yield the best results. However, this method requires no little skill, and as Hakstian (1971) found, it is generally no better than and sometimes less effective than Direct Oblimin.

These rotational procedures try to attain simple structure by maximising the hyperplane count. Hyperplanes are boundaries alongside factors. If these are fixed at + or −0.05 (regarding all loadings within these boundaries as zero) then the hyperplane count is the number of loadings within these hyperplanes. Maximising this maximises the number of zero loadings which is an important criterion of simple structure.

The technically sound factor analysis

From this discussion the technically sound factor analysis can now be described. There will be proper sampling of variables and subjects. After principal factor analysis (or possibly maximum likelihood analysis), the significant factors as selected by the Scree or Velicer tests (or possibly from the maximum likelihood analysis) will be rotated using Direct Oblimin. These simple structure factors will be replicable and should account for much of the variance in the matrix.

In addition to the fact that simple structure factors are replicable and conform to the notion of parsimony, as has been argued, Cattell (1978) contends that they are causal determiners. This argument rests on two points. If random data are factored, simple structure, as defined by the hyperplane count, cannot be obtained. More importantly if artificial data sets with known determiners are factored, simple structure analysis reveals them, as is exemplified in the study of the behaviour of balls. Here three factors emerged: weight, size and elasticity. This makes it clear that simple structure factors are not algebraic artifacts.

Now that the characteristics of good factor analyses have been described, it will be possible in the subsequent chapters of this book to scrutinise critically the psychometric studies of personality which appear to have produced a plethora of contradictory findings. Much of this research will be found wanting, not only with reference to inadequate factor analyses but also in respect of poor tests, as discussed in Chapter 2, and thus results may be ignored.

However, before we turn to an examination of the substantive work in the psychometrics of personality a few other points about factor analyses should be made.

Factor structure and factor pattern

In oblique analyses a factor pattern and a factor structure are produced which in almost all cases are highly similar. In orthogonal rotations, pattern and structure are identical. Structure loadings are the correlations of the variables with the factors. This is the definition of factor loadings given earlier in this chapter. The pattern loadings are beta weights indicating the importance of each variable in predicting the factors. The structure loadings are more stable from study to study and the factor structure should be the basis of the interpretation in oblique analyses.

Confirmatory factor analyses Most factor analyses in the field of personality are exploratory analyses. However, on occasions it is desirable to test hypotheses, and for this confirmatory factor analysis is used. For this there are two possible methods and these will be briefly described.

Procrustes rotations to target matrices In this method a target matrix of loadings is specified on the basis of theory or previous findings and a Procrustes analysis is computed which aims not at simple structure but to match this target matrix as closely as possible. The more precisely the target matrix is specified the more difficult it is to fit, the loadings of simply zero, positive or negative are regarded as an easy target. Guilford (1967) has been the leading exponent of this technique in his studies of human abilities.

This method of hypothesis testing cannot now be supported since Horn and Knapp (1973) showed that target rejection was most unlikely unless the target matrix was specified in detail. They further demonstrated that Procrustes could match target matrices with random data and with data in which hypotheses antithetical to the target were built in. Since, in addition, simple structure factors are preferred because they are simple, the status of Procrustes factors, even if the technique could be trusted, is dubious. Much depends here on the theory from which the target matrix was derived, a criticism which applies equally to the maximum likelihood method discussed below.

Maximum likelihood confirmatory analysis This is the favoured method for testing hypotheses through factor analysis since there are statistical tests of fit. However, as Nunnally (1978) has pointed out, the chi-square test of fit finds it difficult to choose between target matrices unless these are grossly different with the result that judgement still enters the procedure.

However, despite its statistical sophistication, confirmatory analysis has yet to yield any powerful substantive findings in the study of personality beyond those from simple structure analyses. If computing time is available, both methods deserve scrutiny.

R technique Most factor analyses are computed on the correlations between variables. This is known as R technique. However, Cattell (1978) describes some other approaches of which the most important for the study of personality are set out below.

P technique Here test scores obtained from one individual are factored.

This can be powerful in the study of motivation and of variables which change over time.

Q technique Here the correlations between people are factored; the factors thereby revealing groups. This is a useful method in clinical psychology for example, where groups might be found differing on critical personality variables.

O technique Here scores from subjects on two occasions are factored. This can be useful in the study of ongoing processes such as psychotherapy or educational methods.

Conclusions

Sufficient has been said about factor analysis to enable readers to follow the evaluations and criticisms of research which will occur throughout the remainder of this book. The critical issue is that of simple structure. Simple structure factors are replicable and are the logical choice from the infinity of possible factors. That they can be causal is also important. They are attained only in technically adequate factor analyses which involve proper sampling of variables and subjects, and the oblique rotation (by Direct Oblimin) of the correct number of factors chosen by the Scree or Velicer tests. Maximum likelihood methods were permissible but their statistical claims should be treated cautiously. Similarly confirmatory factor analyses need careful scrutiny, for their statistics are not highly sensitive.

Chapter 4

The factor analysis of temperament

In this chapter I shall summarise the main findings from the factor analysis of personality questionnaires which is essentially the study of temperament. As should be obvious from Chapters 1 and 3 of this book, there are many and diverse findings both on account of the difficulties of defining what is meant by personality and the problems of factor analysis. In a chapter of this length a careful description of all the factor analytic research would be pointless, since much of it fails to meet even the least stringent of the criteria discussed in the previous chapter.

I shall discuss, therefore, what is generally regarded, in terms of citation and reference, as the best work in the field, most of which as shall be seen is technically sound, even though in some cases, more recent research has shown the results to be not the best factor analytic description of personality.

I shall begin with the work of the great pioneers in this field – Guilford, Cattell and Eysenck – who have produced factors whose psychological meaning is well explicated by research. I shall deal then more briefly with some other factor analytic sets of factors and the work on the 'big five' which were mentioned in the previous chapter. Finally, based on this discussion I shall delineate the factor analytic picture of human temperament, as it appears in 1992.

The work of Guilford

Guilford *et al.* (1976) in their Handbook to the Guilford–Zimmerman Temperament Survey summarise much of the research with the Guilford factors and this most recent account forms the basis of our discussion. However, it should be pointed out that this research was among the earliest factor analytic work in the field of personality much of which is described in detail in Guilford (1959). The Guilford factors are set out below.

G – General activity: energetic, quick vs. slow, deliberate.
R – Restraint: serious minded vs. impulsive.
A – Ascendance: assertive, confident vs. submissive, hesitant.
S – Sociability: friendly, talkative vs. shy, withdrawn.
E – Emotional stability: cheerful, composed vs. gloomy, excitable.
O – Objectivity: tough vs. tender-minded.
F – Friendliness: respect for others vs. hostility, restraint.
T – Thoughtfulness: reflectiveness vs. interest in the outer world.
P – Personal relations: tolerance of people vs. fault-finding.
M – Masculinity: hardboiled, emotionally inexpressive vs. sympathetic, emotional.

There are several important points to be noted about these factors which will be salient to our discussion throughout this chapter and which will be set out below. Before this is done, however, the status of these factors must be emphasised. These ten factors represent, according to Guilford, the ten most important variables in the personality field. It is these factors which should be considered in trying to understand the nature of personality, and develop any theory about its development and origins. The bipolarity of the factors indicates the meaning of the low and high score on the variables.

1 Reliability of the scales. Against the criteria of good tests discussed in Chapter 2 these scales are excellent; internal consistencies are mostly beyond 0.8 and test-retest reliabilities after one year are also high.
2 Certain variables in this list are noteworthy: tough-mindedness; emotional stability; sociability and thoughtfulness. These are common to the work of most factor analysts. It is particularly interesting that sociability and thoughtfulness are separate factors.
3 These factors are orthogonal. The argument concerning the importance of simple structure and the fact that oblique factors were more likely to be simple was discussed in Chapter 3.
4 Validity of the factors. As was pointed out in Chapter 2, it is difficult to demonstrate the validity of personality factors except through studies of construct validity which necessarily involve the consideration of large numbers of investigations. Guilford *et al.* (1976) summarise a considerable body of research in the test handbook but, as has been pointed out by Kline and Barrett (1983) and Kline (1992a), many of the studies cited there have samples too small for reliable conclusions to be drawn. However, there are a few critical studies which illuminate the psychological meaning and scientific status of the Guilford factors and these will be discussed.

Eysenck and Eysenck (1965), in a joint study of the Guilford, Cattell and Eysenck scales (a research which will be discussed later in this chapter when the Cattell and Eysenck scales are scrutinised), attempted to locate the scales in factor space, an efficient method of investigating the validity of factor analytic tests. These authors carried out an oblique (Promax) rotated factor analysis of items in the Guilford, Cattell and Eysenck scales. However, the Guilford factors did not emerge and it was concluded that these factors were not a good account of personality, probably due to the fact of the orthogonal rotation.

However, only eight items per Guilford scale were used (to reduce the size of the computations) which, as has been shown in Chapter 2, must contribute to lowered reliability of the scales. Furthermore, the Promax rotation may not have reached simple structure (there was no Direct Oblimin at this time). Thus this research, although an impressive contribution, was less than definitive through technical deficiencies of the computing facilities when it was undertaken.

Cattell and Gibbons (1968) administered items from the Guilford and Cattell scales to a large sample of students and submitted them to a factor analysis which, as might be expected from these authors, conformed fully to the criteria of technically adequate factor analyses. In addition they performed an orthogonal rotation. They found that the Guilford factors were essentially identical to those of Cattell when rotated to the oblique position, the majority aligning with the Cattell factors although some were a mixture. Since they could not replicate the Guilford factors orthogonally, they concluded that the Guilford set were no different from those of Cattell but were improperly rotated. However, this conclusion must be discussed again when the Cattell factors are examined, since there is considerable doubt about their structure (see Kline, 1992a).

A study by Amelang and Borkenau (1982) must be mentioned. More will be said about the relationship of the big five factors to other sets of factors at the end of this chapter.

Conclusions concerning the Guilford set of factors

These factors are among the most interesting personality factors since they have their origins in the first factor analyses of personality. However, despite the attractiveness of some of the variables, in terms of common human experience (see G and M, for example) and the fact that the scales are reliable, it is difficult to argue that these factors offer the best possible factor analytic description of temperament. The fact that they are orthogonal is *a priori* somewhat unlikely. There is no personality theory which suggests that the most important personality dimensions might be independent of each other. Furthermore even orthogonal rotations find it difficult to locate the factors, whereas rotated to oblique positions, the factors do not seem independent of other systems. In brief, a brilliant early attempt to factor personality traits but not probably the most parsimonious or meaningful factors that could be produced.

The Cattell factors

Cattell has been, without question, one of the most influential psychologists in the world and since much of his enormous output has been concerned with the factor analysis of personality, his findings must be scrutinised with the utmost care. To summarise 40 or so books and about 550 papers and chapters in one part of a chapter is impossible, but the essentials of his empirical work can be set out. His theoretical account of personality which is more complex will be discussed in Chapter 9.

This summary of Cattell is derived from a study of most of his work but the most important single reference is Cattell (1981) which contains an account of much of the empirical work and theory but is, by any standards, a difficult book. Cattell and Kline (1977) is a more readable discussion of his work and other important books and papers will be cited at relevant points in the description.

The normal Cattell personality factors

These are measured in the 16PF Test (Cattell, Eber and Tatsuoko, 1970) and in versions of the same test for adolescents (High School Personality Questionnaire), primary school children (Children's Personality Questionnaire) and even pre-schoolers (The Pre-school Personality Quiz). Details of all these tests can be found in Cattell (1973) and Kline (1992a). These different tests allow longitudinal studies of the factors and research into the influence of environmental factors on development.

As the name of the test implies, sixteen personality factors are claimed by Cattell to account for much of the variance among personality traits among adults, although there are seven other smaller factors (Cattell, 1973). These sixteen factors are:

A – Reserved, detached vs. outgoing, warmhearted.
B – Crystallised intelligence.
C – Emotionally unstable vs. emotionally stable.
E – Humble, mild vs. assertive, dominant.

F – Sober, taciturn vs. happy-go-lucky, enthusiastic.
G – Expedient, disregards rules vs. conscientious, persistent.
H – Shy, timid vs. venturesome, uninhibited.
I – Tough-minded, self-reliant vs. tender-minded, sensitive.
L – Trusting vs. suspicious.
M – Practical vs. imaginative, bohemian.
N – Forthright, artless vs. shrewd, acute.
O – Self-assured, secure vs. guilt-prone, apprehensive.
Q1 – Conservative vs. radical.
Q2 – Group dependent vs. self-sufficient.
Q3 – Undisciplined, lax vs. controlled.
Q4 – Relaxed, tranquil vs. tense, frustrated.

These primary factors are oblique and at the second-order four factors are extracted:

1 – Introversion vs. extràversion (exvia in Cattell's terminology).
2 – Low anxiety vs. high anxiety.
3 – Sensitivity vs. tough poise.
4 – Dependence vs. independence.

Abnormal factors

Before discussing this factor structure which is claimed by Cattell to set out the major dimensions of personality and which forms the basis of his theorising (Cattell, 1981), it should be pointed out that Cattell has also identified a number of abnormal personality factors which are measured in the *Clinical Analysis Questionnaire* (Krug, 1980). These factors are:

D1. Hypochondriasis. D2. Suicidal depression. D3. Agitation.
D4. Anxious depression. D5. Low energy depression.
D6. Guilt and resentment. D7. Boredom and withdrawal.
Pa. Paranoia. Pp. Psychopathic deviation. Sc. Schizophrenia.
As. Psychasthenia. Ps. Psychological inadequacy.

Discussion of abnormal factors

Because these abnormal factors are a minor part of Cattell's work, I shall discuss them briefly at this point before scrutinising the factor structure of normal personality traits.

These factors are just about reliable enough to use with individuals, having reliabilities around 0.7. However, their validity is less well attested.

Kameoka (1986) examined the factor structure in a sample of students, utilising an oblique Maxplane and Rotoplot analysis (see Chapter 3) as advocated by Cattell (1978). He was able to find the twelve factors although the correlations among the depression factors were larger than expected. It should be noted, however, that this study was among normals and thus the variance would be restricted.

The CAQ is interesting in that it suggests that twelve factors can account for abnormal personality. Furthermore the fact that there are seven depression factors is obviously of interest to clinical and medical psychology. Clearly these factors require much further research but they indicate how factor analysis can illuminate complex fields of psychology.

Discussion of the Cattell normal factors

The Cattell factors are so much more than factors derived from a set of personality test items that it is necessary, if the claims of Cattell concerning the importance of these factors are to be understood, to describe their provenance and the external evidence for their psychological meaning.

Origins of the factors In Chapter 3 it was argued that in exploratory factor analysis, proper sampling of variables was essential. In the development of the 16PF Test, Cattell tried to ensure this by basing his items on a previous analysis of ratings of personality. Originally Cattell searched the dictionary for descriptions of personality, eliminated synonyms, and then rated subjects on all remaining descriptors. These terms were said to embrace the whole of personality – the semantic personality sphere – since existence is dependent on descriptors. We live indeed in a linguistic world (see Cattell, 1957 for a detailed description of this aspect of the research).

Factor analysis of these ratings had revealed twelve L (life) factors and thus Cattell aimed to develop his questionnaires to measure these L factors since by so doing these would also embrace all personality. The end result of this work was the 16PF Test which measured the twelve L factors plus four factors which regularly occurred among items Q1 to Q4. This, grossly simplified, is the basis for Cattell's claim that his factors embrace all personality. He is certainly the first factor analyst to attempt to sample the whole field of personality traits, although it must be pointed out that it is likely that his initial reduction of the personality sphere, necessary given the computational difficulties of factor analysis at that time, were too severe.

Reliability of the scales The reliability of the scales is far from satisfactory. Ten of the sixteen scales have reliabilities lower than 0.7, which is, as has been seen, the usually accepted minimum. Furthermore the parallel forms of the test have low reliabilities, thus making it difficult to regard them as equivalent.

Simple structure Cattell (e.g. 1978) has been responsible for many of the arguments in favour of simple structure rotations and he and his colleagues have developed many of the statistical methods involved. Consequently the factor analytic procedures are technically extremely good, although, as will be argued later in this chapter, other researchers have found it difficult to replicate the factors.

Clinical evidence There is considerable clinical evidence, such as the scores of different neurotic groups, in support of the construct validity of the scales. This research can be found summarised in the handbook to the test (Cattell *Eber and Tatsuoko*, 1970). This will be discussed in Chapter 9 of this book where the application of the psychometric view of personality is scrutinised.

Occupational evidence There is also considerable support for the validity of the test from occupational differences on the sixteen scales and from correlations with occupational success. These factors are widely used both in Great Britain and America in personnel selection (see Herriot, 1989). These results will again be discussed in some detail in Chapter 9.

Educational evidence From educational studies there is some support for the validity of these Cattell factors, notably in the correlations with academic success. Introverts tend to do better at higher education as do mildly anxious students, presumably because they worry if they do not do well.

Genetic factors There is a good body of evidence suggesting that these personality factors are considerably determined by genetic factors. This evidence has come from biometric studies of the personality factors and Cattell (1982) has again been a pioneer in the complex mathematical analyses demanded by biometric methods: work discussed in Chapter 7.

Construct validity It is obvious from the assembly of all these points that there is a huge body of research evidence in favour of these Cattell factors which, given their origins, would seem to support Cattell's claims that these are the definitive factor analytic, psychometric description of personality, and colleagues of Cattell at Illinois, and lately in Hawaii, do strongly articulate this case, as exemplified by Cattell and Johnson (1986). Nevertheless it has to be said that few outside his group are convinced.

There are many reasons for this divergence of views. Some are relatively trivial. Thus it is clear that many psychologists who neglect the work are not prepared to master the multivariate statistical methods which underpin it and are thus unable to follow the arguments concerning rotational procedures, just for example. Furthermore, Cattell invents neologisms to describe his factors because he does not want their meaning to be confused by the connotation of words in everyday use. These again create confusion to those outside the system.

However, there are some more substantive reasons and these must now be discussed. It has always been found difficult by researchers not associated with Cattell to reproduce the Cattell factors. As was mentioned in the previous discussion of the Guilford factors, Eysenck and Eysenck (1969) failed to reproduce the Cattell set. However, Cattell (1973, 1978) put these failures down to inadequacies in the factor analytic methods used; problems which were discussed in the previous chapter. The present writer was convinced by these arguments until together with Paul Barrett he undertook a number of factor analytic studies of questionnaires including the 16PF and EPQ (Eysenck and Eysenck, 1975) tests; work reported in Kline and Barrett (1983).

They found that simple structure analyses of the Cattell factors yielded only seven factors and these were made up of items from a variety of the Cattell factors. Furthermore many items loaded on more than one factor. At the second-order two factors were clear-cut, – anxiety and extraversion. They were forced to conclude that the sixteen factors postulated by Cattell were not the most parsimonious or elegant description of the personality sphere.

A few comments should be made about this study. We were careful to ensure that it reached the technical standards advocated by Cattell. Thus there was a high ratio of subjects to variables and the number of factors was selected by the Scree test. The most efficient oblique rotations were used, as found by Hakstian (1971), and the hyperplane count was tested (all procedures discussed in Chapter 3). Indeed confirmatory analysis was employed to attempt to find sixteen factors. Finally it should be pointed out that the EPQ was subjected to these same techniques and three factors were found as predicted; work discussed later in this chapter.

As has been indicated, the 16PF test embodying Cattell's factors represents the results of the largest research programme into the psychometrics of personality which has ever been devised and it has been conducted with almost unequalled technical brilliance. How is it, therefore, that it now appears that the factor structure of the test is wrong?

There are several reasons which might account for this and these must be briefly discussed. First it could well be the case, as Howarth (1976) has argued, that the twelve life factors based on the ratings were incorrectly identified. This work was carried out before the introduction of computers and utilised cluster analysis, a simplified form of factor analysis. Such an error would be reflected in the 16PF test which was aimed at the L factors.

This argument is supported by the fact that, as has been seen, modern studies of ratings yield the big five factors (McCrae and Costa, 1987) and more recent factorisations of the Cattell and other test items by Noller *et al.* (1987), Boyle (1989) and Amelang and Borkenau (1982) have all concluded that much of the reliable variance in the 16PF test is taken up by these five factors. This work will be further discussed later in this chapter.

In addition, as was argued above, it is possible that the semantic personality sphere was too constricted before ratings were begun.

In brief, therefore, it may well be that the failure to replicate the sixteen factors in the Cattell system arises from the fact that the whole basis of the analysis was wrong. Certainly it is the case that if the original factor analyses of the 16PF are examined (see Cattell, 1957), Cattell was prepared to accept rather low loadings as evidence that the correct variables loaded the factors.

If, however, these arguments are accepted it is still necessary to explain why it is so widely used in occupational selection. As has been fully discussed in Kline (1992a), there are several reasons to account for this anomaly. First, the two largest second-orders, extraversion and anxiety, are present in the 16PF, as are short scales of tough-mindedness (I) and conventionality (G) which are also part of the big five. Thus the influence of these factors may account for the multiple correlations between the factors and occupational success. Secondly, on sixteen scales it would be surprising if there were not some differences between occupational groups. Since there are few good theories of occupational choice it is not difficult to develop reasonable convincing *post hoc* arguments for the results. The third argument concerns the scientific naïveté of most occupational selection processes. Applicants are selected and if found satisfactory it is assumed that the selection methods were adequate. However, there is no follow-up of those who were rejected. Indeed it may well be the case that in management jobs, where all applicants are highly qualified and well-experienced, it would matter little which were taken on the payroll.

Conclusions

From all these arguments it must be concluded that the sixteen Cattell factors do not represent the most simple and efficient factor analytic description of personality. This is not to denigrate the contribution of Cattell to this field. His contribution to the factor analysis of personality showed how the subject should be tackled and his advances in methodology have enhanced the whole of psychometrics.

The Objective Analytic Test Battery (OAB) (Cattell and Schuerger, 1976)

Before leaving the work of Cattell on temperament, a little more needs to be said about the OAB, which was mentioned in Chapter 2 as being one of the few published objective tests. I shall not say much about it because the study by Kline and Cooper (1984b) demonstrated that it was not a valid test, at least in Great Britain. Nevertheless it deserves a brief description here if only because of its ingenuity and originality.

It claims to measure ten source traits: self-assertion, independence, evasiveness, exuberance, regression, anxiety, realism, self-assurance, exvia (extraversion) and discouragement.

There is a huge number of objective subtests which are too numerous to describe in detail here but include, for example: estimates of how good performances are; rapid calculations of arithmetic; picture memory; human nature where subjects indicate their agreement with common beliefs about people; how long does it take? – where subjects indicate how long they would take to do certain things.

It is clear that this is an ingenious and truly objective test in that deliberate faking is virtually impossible. However, because there is little support for its validity, I shall say no more about the OAB (more details may be found in Kline, 1992a) but pass on to the work of Eysenck.

The work of Eysenck

Eysenck, like Cattell, has made a huge contribution to the psychometric study of personality. He has more than 1,000 publications to his credit but the publications most relevant to this chapter are Eysenck (1967) and Eysenck and Eysenck (1976), although other research will be cited as necessary.

Eysenck, over the years, has produced a number of personality tests, each an improvement on the one before. Thus there was the original

Maudsley Medical Questionnaire which measured neuroticism (N), the Maudsley Personality Inventory measuring extraversion (E) and neuroticism, as did the Eysenck Personality Inventory and the more recent Eysenck Personality Questionnaire, the EPQ (Eysenck and Eysenck, 1975) which was the definitive measure of the Eysenck factors, extraversion, neuroticism and psychoticism (P). However, in 1992 a yet newer version has been produced, the EPQR (Eysenck *et al.*, 1992). However, since almost all the research into the nature of these factors has been conducted with the EPQ I shall describe this test although the new aspects of the EPQR will be discussed at the end of this section.

The original basis of the N factor was ratings of patients suffering from neurotic disorders. These were factored and an N factor emerged which was measured in the MMQ. The extraversion factor had its origins in the study of the Guilford factors and the psychoticism factor had been observed in studies of abnormal subjects, particularly psychotic patients and certain criminal offenders, but was only successfully put into questionnaire form in the EPQ. Descriptions of the basic research, culminating in these EPQ factors, can be found in Eysenck (1967) and Eysenck and Eysenck (1976).

In this section I shall describe the EPQ because this is the measure of the factors which has been used in attempts to validate them and to explore their psychological significance. I shall then summarise this research into the nature of the EPQ factors which distinguishes the work of Eysenck from most factor analysts (except of course Cattell), who are content to produce tests. It is this research which gives psychological meaning to the EPQ variables and ensures that the factors are far more than sets of homogeneous items.

The Eysenck Personality Questionnaire

Four variables are measured, as set out below:

1 Extraversion–introversion. The extravert is cheerful, sociable, outward looking while the introvert is withdrawn, quiet and inhibited.
2 Neuroticism. The high neurotic is worrying and anxious, the low scorer the opposite of this.
3 Psychoticism. The high scorer is tough-minded, ruthless, likes powerful sensations and lacks empathy. Criminals are high scorers and males are higher than females. In the EPQ, normals scored very low on this factor but this distribution has been improved on the recent EPQR, thus allowing more precise factor analytic studies with normal populations.
4 Lie scale. This screens out those who give socially desirable responses.

Reliabilities The internal consistency reliabilities of these scales are all beyond 0.7 and test-retest reliabilities are also beyond this figure except for the P scale; this latter caused by the low scores of females on this variable. For a personality questionnaire these reliability coefficients are excellent.

Validity of the scales These are unquestionably the best validated factors in the psychometrics of personality. This arises from the extensive experimental work of Eysenck and colleagues, as well as many other psychologists, into the nature of these factors. This research will be summarised under a number of headings.

1. Factor structure There can be no doubt that the factor structure of the EPQ is exactly as it should be with each of the N, P, E and L items loading their respective scales. Thus Kline and Barrett (1983) demonstrated in a simple structure oblique rotation of the intercorrelations between the virtually perfect separation of N, E and P items. Factor loadings were high and the construct validity of N, E and P was supported most strongly. Helmes (1989), a specialist in the factor structure of the EPQ, subjected the items to a confirmatory analysis, the target matrix being derived from the marking key. He confirmed the results of Kline and Barrett (1983), although some of the P items were weak, because of their low endorsement rate, a failing which was mentioned above and which has been remedied in the EPQR.

Thus there are three clear factors in the EPQ. Their psychological nature has been determined by research described below.

2. Physiology Eysenck (1967) has described the physiological basis of these factors. Extraversion has been related to the arousability of the central nervous system, neuroticism to the lability of the autonomic nervous system and psychoticism to androgen level. The extravert is lowly aroused. This accounts for the fact that extraverts enjoy noisy situations such as pubs and parties and are highly sociable. This is why extraverts are easily bored and cannot stand monotony. Without noise the extravert is likely to nod off. Introverts who like quiet pursuits, such as reading and thinking, are always highly aroused and further environmental stimulation is simply too much. In the occupational field, for example, it has been shown that extraverts are poor at monotonous tasks, making errors and that introverts should be selected for them. Many of the correlates of extraversion are to be found in Eysenck (1970).

The autonomic nervous system controls involuntary responses such as heart rate, sweating, digestion and the dissemination of hormones throughout the body. Lability means that this system is easily activated and then inhibited, what is called sympathetic and parasympathetic activity. That this is involved in the neuroticism or anxiety factor is no surprise. The rapid mood swings, the stomach contractions, pallor and sweating, all associated with anxiety, make this hypothesis likely. Thus the individual high on neuroticism has a highly labile system whereas the stolid, phlegmatic low scorer has an autonomic system which does not much fluctuate. Eysenck (1967) contains much of this physiological evidence.

The physiology of P has not been studied to the same extent as the other variables and the implication of high androgen level in high P scorers is considered to be more of a tenable hypothesis than one confirmed by an overwhelming body of evidence. However, the sex differences and the fact, that many traditionally feminine characteristics, especially empathy and tender-mindedness (see Guilford's masculinity factor), load this factor, make this hypothesis not unlikely.

3. Heritability of E, N and P. Eaves *et al.* (1989) showed in a study of 500 twins using biometric analysis that these variables had a high heritability index with about 70 per cent of the population variance being determined by genetic factors. This and other similar work will be discussed in Chapter 7 on the heritability of personality where the significance of the findings for personality theory will be examined. Here, however, it is sufficient to point out that the fact that these factors are strongly genetically determined means that it is unlikely that they are simply statistical artifacts of the factor analysis. High heritability indices always confer psychological significance on variables.

Here, it should be pointed out that in factor analysis a factor may always be produced if sufficient similar items are included in a test. Cattell (1973) refers to such factors as bloated specifics. This is why in our discussion of factor analysis, it was argued that all emerging factors, even from simple structure analyses, should be identified with reference to some external criterion. Bloated specifics could never have high heritability indices.

4. External criteria The Eysenck factors are related to a wide variety of external criteria in accord with their claimed psychological characteristics. These findings are fully discussed in Chapter 8 on the application of psychometric personality factors in clinical, educational and occupational psychology. Here it is sufficient, as a demonstration of the construct validity of the factors, to note some of the most important results, namely that these factors are implicated in neurosis (Eysenck, 1961), smoking, criminality, political allegiance and school learning (see Modgil and Modgil, 1986, for interesting summary discussions of many of these and similar issues).

Conclusions concerning the Eysenck factors

All these lines of evidence – the replicable clarity of the factor structure, the correlations with external variables, the high heritability indices and the clear implication of physiological structures – firmly support the validity and psychological importance of these factors.

This conclusion receives further support from the survey of normal factors in questionnaires by Kline and Barrett (1983) who argued that these three factors and a fourth one of obsessionality were the only clear and replicable factors to be found. More recent work on the big five personality factors confirms this view, where these three factors are seen as three of the big five (McCrae and John, in press); work to be discussed at the end of this chapter.

The factors which have so far been discussed have emerged from the pioneers in the field of the factor analysis of personality, whose factors have been investigated, as has been seen, in respect of a wide variety of external criteria. However, from the many other factor analysts, who have provided their own sets of factors, I shall briefly describe the work of Comrey, who attempted to improve the psychometric characteristics of personality inventories and whose factors are highly reliable and stable, and work on the big five factors, research which has been mentioned throughout this chapter.

The Comrey factors

Comrey (1970) developed a new set of factors precisely because there was so little agreement between the factors advocated by Cattell, Eysenck and Guilford and because he considered that, as has been argued, there were psychometric deficiencies in their scales. The factors in the Comrey scales are:

Trust vs. Defensiveness
Social conformity vs. Rebelliousness
Emotional stability vs. Neuroticism
Empathy vs. Egocentrism
Orderliness vs. Lack of compulsion
Activity vs. Lack of energy
Masculinity vs. Femininity

Extraversion vs. Introversion

The reliability of the scales is high, all beyond 0.8, and the scales cannot be faulted on this point.

Comments on the Comrey factors

One of the weaknesses of many scales, according to Comrey, resided in the fact that the individual items were unreliable, being either trichotomous or dichotomous. This was remedied in the Comrey scales by using seven point rating scales for responses and by factoring the correlations between subsets of similar items (factored homogeneous item dimensions, FHIDs) rather than individual items. This certainly accounts for the high reliabilities.

Examination of the scales suggests that the main factors are measured in this test. Thus extraversion, neuroticism (or anxiety), tough-mindedness and conformity can all be found. Clearly the variance cannot be much different from that of the three scales which have been scrutinised in this chapter.

Cattell (1978) has criticised the rotational methods used by Comrey in this test as being unlikely to reach simple structure and it is interesting to examine the joint analyses of this test with the other important personality factors. Thus Cattell (1973), citing research by Barton, claimed that the Comrey factors were not simple structure factors but that there was good agreement between them and the Cattell second-orders. Noller *et al.* (1987) factored the Comrey, Cattell and Eysenck factors, using Comrey's unusual rotational procedures, and found only seven factors, five of which appeared to be the big five factors which have been mentioned throughout this chapter. Boyle (1989) essentially confirmed the big five factors with the same data but using more orthodox methods.

Conclusions

These Comrey factors are stable and reliable but are almost certainly not simple structure factors. The variance in the test is highly similar to that of the other personality questionnaires but at best, re-rotated, it measures the largest second-order factors in the personality test realm. As they stand the Comrey factors are not the simplest and most elegant personality factors.

The big five factors

From this discussion of the most important psychometric factor analytic studies of personality, it has become evident that what are usually referred to as the big five factors have been claimed by various researchers to underlie the variance in all these tests. In other words the best factor analytic description of personality is that there are five personality factors and that most tests even when they were not designed specifically to measure these factors in fact do so. To conclude this chapter, therefore, I shall examine the evidence for postulating the big five.

Description of the big five factors

1 Extraversion.
2 Agreeableness.
3 Conscientiousness.
4 Neuroticism.
5 Openness to experience.

These are the names given to these factors by McCrae and John (in press) in their most recent account of the system, although, as has been seen, other names are sometimes used. For example, agreeableness is similar to tender- vs. tough- mindedness and openness to experience equates with conventionality. The precise names are not important compared with the identity of the factors in the various studies. As these authors argue, these factors have been found in self-reports, ratings, natural languages, theoretically-based questionnaires, English, Dutch, German and Japanese adult samples (John, 1990). In addition they appear to endure across decades in adults (McCrae and Costa, 1990).

Tupes and Christal (1961) noted that five factors seemed to emerge from studies of personality in which ratings were involved; a claim that was supported by Norman (1963). Goldberg (1983) also showed that analysis of descriptive terms in natural language seemed to reveal about five factors. This analysis of natural language was, as has been seen, the original basis of Cattell's 16PF test. Furthermore, analysis of the leading personality tests also seemed to reveal that about five factors accounted for the reliable variance. McCrae and Costa in various studies have been responsible for much of this work. Thus the big five were to be found in the Eysenck scales (McCrae and Costa, 1985), the Guilford scales (Amelang and Borkenau, 1982), the Comrey and Cattell scales (Noller *et al.*, 1987), the Myers–Briggs Type Indicator (McCrae and Costa, 1989a), the MMPI (Costa *et al.*, 1986), the Personality Research Form (Costa and McCrae,

1988), the last three tests being described in Chapter 5, and even in a test of vocational interests, the Holland Vocational Preference Inventory (Holland, 1985).

Such a consensus, from ratings, factor analytic and other personality tests has led not only the main proponents of the big five, Costa and McCrae, to claim that these factors underlie the factors among personality traits, but other researchers in this field have accepted this view (e.g. Digman, 1990). Where there is agreement among different tests and with different statistical methods, it seems difficult to reject the claims. Imperfect rotational procedures, for example, add in error and are most unlikely to result in such striking agreement. Certainly it is not difficult with questionnaire items to find a five-factor structure as Kline and Lapham (1991) showed in the development of the PPQ, a personality test for occupational selection and designed to measure these big five factors.

NEO Personality Inventory (Costa and McCrae, in press)

Devised by McCrae and Costa, this NEO ought to be the supreme personality inventory. Its rationale springs from the findings that five factors are common to ratings, natural language and inventories and it seems as our references demonstrate to measure the big five factors. Certainly these test constructors should be measuring the right variables.

Reliability of the scales

This is sufficiently high, all beyond 0.7, to make the test psychometrically efficient.

Evidence for validity

The evidence for the validity of these scales has been discussed. It resides in the factor analytic studies with other tests. However, as has been argued by Kline (1992a), this evidence is not quite as strong as it first appears. Thus it could be the case that these factors in the NEO did account for the variance in other tests but that they were not the factors claimed by the authors.

This need for external validation of the factors was answered to some extent by an ingenious factor analytic study in which in a sample of nearly 1,000 subjects the NEO factors were located in factor space relative to a form of the NEO completed by peers and spouses (observations by others on the NEO items), adjective check lists and biographical factors (McCrae and Costa, 1989b).

However, a form of Procrustes rotation was used which has been shown to be able to hit target matrices in random data and correlations with other similar measures are not as convincing as are correlations with criteria beyond the domain of tests.

Conclusions

There is little doubt that the NEO inventory is about the best measure of the big five factors, which are clearly implicated in the factor analytic personality tests which have been described in this chapter. Similar factors appear in ratings and natural languages. Nevertheless, the validity of these NEO scales is not supported by correlations with external criteria, as is the case with the EPQ measures of these factors. This, of course, is a much newer test and it is to be hoped that such research will be pursued.

Thus from this survey of the factor analytic study of personality there is a powerful case for three factors: extraversion, anxiety or neuroticism and tough mindedness, all with convincing external validity. The two other factors, openness to experience and conscientiousness, are well supported in the realm of questionnaires, although their independence (they may be aspects of obsessionality, see Kline and Barrett, 1983) needs further research, as do their external correlates.

In Chapter 5 I shall consider the findings from personality tests constructed by methods other than factor analysis, since their findings must also form part of the psychometric view of personality.

Chapter 5

Findings from other types of psychometric tests

Although factor analysis has been the statistical method which has led to the establishment of clear factors in the field of personality, as was demonstrated in the previous chapter, nevertheless, as was pointed out in Chapter 2, tests can be developed by other methods, not involving factors. In this present chapter the substantive findings from the best tests of this kind, all of course aspects of the psychometric view of personality, will be considered.

Minnesota Multiphasic Personality Inventory, the MMPI (Hathaway and McKinley, 1951)

I shall begin with a study of the research with the personality questionnaire, which is undoubtedly the most widely used and researched of all inventories, there being more than 10,000 published articles, books and chapters about this test, let alone unpublished doctoral dissertations (Eysenck, 1989). Recently, however, there has been a substantial revision of this test – the MMPI–2 (Graham,1990) – and this will also be discussed. However, since this is so recent, most of the discussion will refer to the older test except where specifically stated.

Basic information about the test

- The scales were constructed by the criterion keyed-method, i.e. items were selected if they could discriminate clinical groups, a method of test construction discussed in Chapter 2.
- Nine clinical variables are measured by the basic MMPI although more than 200 other scales have been developed (Dahlstrom and Walsh, 1960). These are:

Hs. Hypochondriasis; D. Depression; Hy. Hysteria;
Pd. Psychopathic deviate; Mf. Masculinity/Femininity;
Pa. Paranoia; Pt. Psychasthenia; Sc. Schizophrenia; Ma. Hypomania
Si. Social introversion.

— The test contains 566 items of the 'True'/'False' variety. However, various short versions of the test have been developed.

— Reliabilities. The internal consistency reliabilities of these scales are far too low for psychometric efficiency. Certainly they are not homogeneous, as Graham (1990) makes clear.

Discussion of the test

Clearly 10,000 published studies could not be fully examined even in a large book. However, I shall concentrate upon those researches critical to the thesis of this chapter, namely those which bear on the substantive findings from the test. Before this can be done, however, it is necessary to discuss a number of difficulties with this test, problems which render many of the findings somewhat dubious. In fact, many of these have been dealt with elsewhere in this book (Chapter 2) and thus they can be briefly listed here.

The first problem concerns the criterion-keyed method of test construction, which, as has been argued, leads to scales of little psychological meaning since the criterion groups may differ on a number of variables. This makes the psychological interpretation of research findings difficult. This method also allows the same items to appear in different scales. When this occurs, correlational and factor analyses are difficult to interpret for obvious reasons.

The low reliability of the scales was mentioned, a phenomenon which is always likely with criterion-keyed tests and which highlights again the lack of homogeneity and thus meaning of the scales.

There is a further difficulty with the MMPI which stems from the fact that it was developed as a clinical instrument for use with abnormal subjects. While the test discriminates among abnormal groups, mainly because many of the items refer to neurotic symptoms, when it is administered to normal subjects there is far less variance and scores on the scales tend to be low. Most normal individuals, by definition, have less symptoms than those receiving psychiatric treatment. As was made clear from Chapter 3 on factor analysis, a lack of variance affects the clarity of the emerging factors.

These problems are not such that it is impossible to investigate the psychological meaning of the MMPI but they do make research more difficult and the results have to be treated with some caution.

The simplest approach to uncovering the psychological meaning of the MMPI is to factor analyse the items (rather than the scales which are probably not unifactorial) in the test. With 566 items more than 1,000 subjects would be required for a sound factor analysis, from the viewpoint of subject numbers, as was discussed in Chapter 3 when the criteria of good analyses were set out. This is important because many of the factor analytic studies of the MMPI items fail to achieve simple structure, thus making their results of dubious worth.

However, the investigation by Johnson *et al.* (1984) should be mentioned since it involved 11,000 subjects, thus reducing statistical error to a minimum. Twenty-one factors emerged which were named from the items loading on them, although it must be noted that there was no external validity for their identification. The factors included: anxiety, psychoticism, extraversion, paranoia, psychopathic deviation and psychasthenia. These six factors have been selected because the first three factors have the same names as three of the big five factors discussed in the previous chapter, although it must be stressed that there is no empirical evidence that they are those factors. The last three are similar to the three of the abnormal Cattell factors found by Krug (1980), mentioned in the previous chapter and forming a part of the CAQ. Despite the large numbers of subjects and the fact that there appears to be some similarity with well-established factors, this study by Johnson *et al.* (1984) does not provide a definitive factor structure of these MMPI items however, partly because there is no external validation of the factors.

Costa *et al.* (1985, 1986) carried out a factor analysis of the MMPI items in a large sample of non-psychiatric patients and attempted to relate the emerging factors to other scales, thus validating, to some extent, the factor labels. Nine factors emerged: neuroticism, psychoticism, masculinity, extraversion, religious orthodoxy, somatic complaints, inadequacy, cynicism and intellectual interests. These factors were correlated with the big five and Costa *et al.* (1986) argued that these were to be found in the MMPI variance. Two points should be noted about this conclusion. If it is the case that the big five factors are to be found in the MMPI items, they can certainly be measured more efficiently by other tests. However, there is some other variance in the MMPI, probably related to abnormal personality, and this needs further clarification.

In the CAQ (Krug, 1980) the factors found by Cattell and Bolton (1969) in their study of the MMPI items were incorporated into the test. These were: paranoia, psychopathic deviation, schizophrenia, psychological inadequacy and psychasthenia. These however, although clearly marked as factors, still require external validation before they could be regarded as substantive factors of abnormal personality. Nevertheless they demand research.

Conclusions from factor analyses of MMPI items

The factors derived from the MMPI items are of two kinds, normal and abnormal, as might be expected from a personality test derived from discriminations among clinical groups. The normal factors are probably similar to the big five while the abnormal factors require external validation, although it should be said that the paranoia, psychasthenia and psychopathic deviation factors seem to replicate well and make good psychological sense.

Factoring the MMPI scales

It might appear more simple to factor the MMPI scales rather than the items and indeed this has frequently been done. However, the difficulty of item overlap, the low reliability of the scales and even selecting which scales to choose of the 200 which have been developed, makes the task somewhat problematic. However, despite these difficulties there is considerable agreement as to the factors in the MMPI scales, as Friedman *et al.* (1989) point out. There are two replicated factors – anxiety and repression. The first of these is not unexpected.

Conclusions

Despite the huge amount of research conducted with the MMPI, it has to be concluded that it has added little to our knowledge of personality. This is because it was developed by criterion analysis of an item pool before factor analysis was generally available. A heroic research effort has resulted in a test which may be useful for screening, but its psychometric inadequacies, its low reliability and lack of a clear factor structure mean that it should after more than half a century be gracefully retired. It is a test developed by outmoded technology.

However, these problems were not unknown to some users of the MMPI and, as was stated above, a new form of the test, the MMPI–2, was developed and this will now be discussed.

MMPI–2 (Butcher, 1990)

This version of the test was developed, according to Graham (1990), to improve the samples from which the original clinical scales were derived, to modify the items some of which were now obsolete in terms of content and to widen the behaviour to which the items referred (e.g. the use of drugs).

It must be noted that these aims do not overcome the deficiencies of the test from the viewpoint of contributing to a knowledge of psychology. Indeed the fact that it was intended that the MMPI–2 resembled the old test as much as possible, but in an improved form, suggests that the lack of a clear factor structure will still reduce the psychological meaning of the scales. In fact, there is still item overlap and although the scales are more reliable than the originals they are far from homogeneous. Although no factor analyses have been carried out, Graham (1990) argues that anxiety and repression are likely to be the main factors in the scales.

In brief it must be concluded that the same objections to the MMPI apply to MMPI–2 and that this test cannot contribute much to the psychometric view of personality.

Tests based upon theories and variables derived from tests

In this section of the chapter I shall consider the findings from two different kinds of personality inventories. First I shall scrutinise two well-known tests which are based upon personality theories, those of Jung and Murray. Then I shall consider the evidence for two apparently important personality variables, which have their origins in personality testing – the authoritarian personality and locus of control.

Most theories of personality, as was made clear in the opening chapter, lack rigorous, scientific evidence in their favour. Many of the most famous theories are clinical, such as the various versions of psychoanalysis, and although appealing, to endorse them as they stand, is strictly irrational. For this reason, tests which measure the variables of such theories are particularly important in the scientific study of personality since if they are validated, this *ipso facto* supports the theory. Thus the scrutiny of the validity of such tests scrutinises these theories.

The Myers–Briggs Type Indicator (Briggs and Myers, 1962)

This test claims to classify individuals according to the Jungian theory of eight personality types and an extended typology (Jung, 1949):

1 Extraverted thinking	2 Introverted thinking
3 Extraverted feeling	4 Introverted feeling
5 Extraverted sensing	6 Introverted sensing
7 Extraverted intuition	8 Introverted intuition

The scales are reasonably reliable and thus all turns upon the validity of the test.

Test validity Some continuous scores are obtainable from this test but these are not relevant to this chapter and I shall ignore the studies of their validity. What is critical is whether this test can classify individuals into meaningful groups which resemble those described by Jung. However, it should be noted that McCrae and Costa (1989) have argued that in fact even in this test much of the variance is accounted for by the big five. This, of course, runs counter to the validity of the test as one of Jungian types, although correlational studies are difficult since some of the scores in the MBTI are ipsative.

Stricker and Ross (1964) examined the distribution of the MBTI scores but found no evidence for typologies of any sort – bimodal rather than continuous distributions of scores would be required. In fact, with multi-determined variables typological rather than continuous distribution would be highly unlikely. In nature typologies are the exception.

Broadway (1964), in a paper which can be found in Vetter and Smith (1971), persuaded twenty-eight Jungian analysts to classify themselves into types and take the MBTI. There was full agreement for introversion and extraversion and better than chance classification for sensation and intuition. It should be noted that this classification was not exactly into the categories above but is acceptable Jungian theory. This appears impressive, especially in respect of introversion–extraversion, but it is by no means conclusive support.

Thus it is quite possible to classify oneself correctly as an introvert or a sensationist without implying typologies of any sort. The classification could simply represent one's position above or below the mean. This is highly important in the case of extraversion since, as has been shown, there is general agreement that there is such a factor. The Jungian concept is quite different involving a typology. Furthermore, we do not know the quality of these Jungian analysts or the extent to which they are a representative sample. Thus these findings are not convincing.

The Dynamic Personality Inventory (Grygier and Grygier, 1976)

A brief mention should be made of this test which attempts to measure Freudian personality variables, e.g. oral and anal characteristics, as described by Freud in his general psychosexual theory.

There are thirty-three Freudian variables which are measured with varying degrees of reliability and which, if shown to be valid, would provide psychometric support for Freudian personality theory. I have reviewed the validity of this test in great detail in Kline (1981, 1992a) and it is sufficient to summarise the results here.

Most of the factor analyses of the DPI cited in the handbook to the test have to be treated with caution because they fall short of the criteria for satisfactory factor analyses. What is required is the location of these Freudian scales in factor space in order to investigate their construct validity. Kline and Storey (1978) attempted this rotating to simple structure the DPI scales together with the Cattell and Eysenck factors (see Chapter 4) and measures of authoritarian personality which are described in a later section of this chapter.

From the viewpoint of this chapter, the interesting finding was that a factor emerged which loaded on the measures of obsessional traits and authoritarian personality, a factor which Kline and Barrett (1983) showed was highly important in questionnaires and which is similar to the conservatism and conscientiousness factors of the big five. It was also clear that the DPI measured quite different factors from those of Eysenck and Cattell, although there was little evidence to support their validity as measures of psychosexual variables. It cannot be said, in brief, that this test provides psychometric confirmation of Freudian theory, or that the factors contribute to the psychometric view of personality.

Jackson Personality Research Form, the PRF (Jackson, 1974)

This test is based upon Murray's (1938) theory of needs and presses which postulates that a large number of needs (of which the PRF measures the twenty most important) account for human behaviour. Thus if this test were shown to be valid, these needs could be said to be part of the psychometric view of personality.

There are various forms of the PRF but I shall discuss the results with Form E which contains all the scales developed by Jackson in the shortest form, and with a vocabulary level suited for general adult use.

The twenty needs of the PRF are: abasement, achievement, affiliation, aggression, autonomy, change, cognitive structure (need for precision), defendence, dominance, endurance, exhibition, harm-avoidance, impulsivity, nurturance, order, play, sentience (need for physical sensations), social recognition, succorance (need for support), understanding. In addition, there are two scales to assess social desirability and careless responding.

Test construction It is generally agreed that the PRF is psychometrically one of the best tests. Given the relatively short scales of Form E, the reliability is high and the item analyses were technically highly sophisticated, as is fully discussed in Kline (1992a), although it is difficult to see why factor analysis was not used. Thus all turns on the validity of these scales. In the manual to the test there is no evidence presented for validity other than correlations with ratings for the other forms of the PRF, which is little more than face validity. Other studies are required.

Nesselroade and Baltes (1975) factored the scales (not the items) in the PRF and the HSPQ (the adolescent version of the Cattell 16PF, discussed in Chapter 4) in a well-conducted research. Eight factors were found, which fact alone fails to support the validity of these PRF needs. Since, as has been argued, the validity of the Cattell factors is itself in doubt, there is no need here to attempt to interpret these factors. In brief, this study did not support the validity of the PRF.

Guthrie *et al.* (1981) factored the PRF in a sample of Filipino students and found six factors, which he claimed were common to American and French samples. Again, this study does not confirm the validity of these scales as measures of twenty independent needs. Finally, as has been noted, Costa and McCrae (1988) found the big five factors in this test, a claim supported by Digman (1990).

Conclusions concerning the PRF Despite the technical expertise in the item analytic construction of the PRF, it has to be said that there is no evidence, as yet, that it is a valid measure of the twenty needs it purports to measure. There appear to be about eight factors, at the second-order, in this test and these are highly similar to the big five factors and the Cattell second-orders. Thus the PRF is essentially measuring what the majority of personality scales measure *inter alia* – the big five factors.

From this it is clear that this test cannot be used to support the Murray system of needs and presses. Furthermore it appears to possess no clear-cut factors of its own which have been externally validated or identified. Thus its positive contribution to the psychometric view of personality is not large, although given its technical expertise the fact that it fails to support the Murray needs is useful negative evidence.

Thus the two most widely used tests, deliberately constructed on the basis of theories of personality, the MBTI and the PRF, are probably not valid and psychometric support for these theories cannot be derived from these tests.

The authoritarian personality

Adorno *et al.* (1950) carried out one of the most famous studies of personality in which a battery of tests of various types were given to fascistic subjects in an effort to discover the psychological basis of fascism and anti-semitism, which at that time, for obvious reasons, were of particular relevance and interest. Although, as Brown (1965) has pointed out, there were considerable methodological problems in this work, the concept of authoritarian personality has lived on and it seems to have considerable explanatory power. The authoritarian, sycophantic to her superiors, ruthless to inferiors, bound by rule and status, only doing her duty, is all too recognisable, in hierarchical organisations. It is they who represent the banality of evil, as Eichmann has been described.

The question which I shall briefly consider in this section, although it is an enormous subject (see, for example, Stone and Lederer, 1991), is whether in the light of modern psychometrics the notion of authoritarian personality is any longer viable. If it is, of course, it is reasonable to regard it as a major contribution from psychometrics and an important aspect of the psychometric view of personality.

As was mentioned above, the original study of the authoritarian personality was criticised on methodological grounds: the F scale which measured authoritarianism was not balanced for yes and no responses, thus allowing the influence of acquiescence to affect its scores; the F scale items were biased by social desirability; the scales measured only right wing authoritarian attitudes; the scores reflected the attitudes of the ignorant ill-educated rather than the specifically fascistic. In response to these criticisms there have been many attempts to produce new authoritarian measures, free of these defects.

Kline and Cooper (1984a) factored a number of authoritarian scales in an attempt to locate the authoritarian personality in factor space. This, it was hoped, would demonstrate whether it was a useful concept or whether the variance was better accounted for by other factors. They showed that there was an authoritarian factor which loaded on measures of obsessional personality and on a measure of anal character. They concluded that the authoritarian personality, was the social, attitudinal emanation of the obsessional personality, the factor which Kline and Barrett (1983) had shown was a large second-order factor among personality questionnaires.

It should be noted, in respect of this analysis of the authoritarian personality, that this obsessional factor is highly similar to the open-mindedness and conventionality of the big five.

Christie (1991) has an excellent review of most of the measures of authoritarian personality and argues that one scale is superior in terms of psychometric qualities and content to other tests of authoritarian personality. This is the Right Wing Authoritarian Scale, the RWA, by Altmeyer (1981), a highly reliable balanced scale, with good evidence of validity. This test has twenty-four items to which subjects respond on a six-point scale – disagree strongly to agree strongly.

Before drawing any conclusions about the authoritarian personality, mention should be made of a highly similar concept – dogmatism (Rokeach, 1960). Rokeach had strongly contended that the authoritarian personality was a right wing form of a more general trait – dogmatism, characterised by rigidity and a mind closed to new ideas which could be found along the whole political spectrum. Rokeach, therefore, developed a forty-item scale to measure rigidity of belief, of high internal consistency but still of unproven validity. Certainly Kline and Cooper (1984a) found that a counterbalanced dogmatism scale (Ray, 1970) correlated only low with a counterbalanced F scale (Kohn, 1972), the scale which loaded highest on the authoritarian factor. The work reported in Rokeach (1960) indicates that dogmatism is an interesting variable. However, the factor analytic research demonstrates that it is not identical with the F scale. It would be useful if the dogmatism scale were rotated to simple structure together with the main personality tests to identify its psychological nature. However, it does not seem to be as important or robust a variable as the authoritarian personality.

Conclusions concerning the authoritarian personality The original study of the authoritarian personality by Adorno *et al.* (1950) was a highly impressive and convincing account of authoritarianism despite the fact that it had psychometric methodological problems. Modern studies of authoritarianism with improved measures support the concept of authoritarian personality. It seems to be the political or attitudinal aspect of the obsessional personality, a syndrome of personality traits typified by the need for self-control, control of others, rigidity and conservatism. This personality concept has been defined and refined by psychometric testing and it must be considered a major contribution from psychometrics to an understanding of personality.

Locus of control

Locus of control is variable which has no immediate referent in everyday language, although there is a large number of psychometric tests which purport to measure it. Thus if any of these were shown to be valid, the concept of locus of control would be a contribution of psychometrics to personality and, as was the case with authoritarian personality, an aspect of the psychometric view of personality.

Locus of control is a concept which originated in social learning theory, as it was developed by Rotter (1966). External locus of control refers to the belief that the external environment rather than personal effort determines what happens. Internal locus of control is the opposite, namely that outcomes are contingent on actions. Locus of control is held to be a personality characteristic or trait which is broadly generalisable across a variety of situations.

Nevertheless, as was pointed out in Kline (1992a), there is a conceptual difficulty with locus of control which renders it of dubious worth although it is widely used in social psychology. Thus Lefcourt (1991), in a chapter which discusses many of the tests of locus of control, argues that measures of locus of control should be tailored to particular populations and concerns and that these specific measures are more efficient than a broad measure of the variable, a viewpoint which the major workers in this field all support (e.g. Phares, 1976; Rotter, 1975). However, if this is the case, it suggests that locus of control is not a broad trait at all, but rather a specific and particular belief and is thus of little psychological interest. An example will clarify this point. The general locus of control dimension reflects a belief that outcomes are determined by external influences at one pole contrasted with personal effort at the other. Thus such a scale should predict such beliefs in fields such as health or success at work. However, in fact this is not so. Specific measures relating to health and relating to work are required. This suggests that there is no general factor and that the variable is relatively trivial psychologically.

It is therefore of considerable interest, given this theoretical argument, to examine the factor structure and the location in factor space of the general locus of control variable, the specific tests being of little theoretical or psychological interest.

Lefcourt (1991) in his lengthy review of tests of locus of control claims that the original locus of control scale (Rotter, 1966) is still the most used and widely cited test so that I shall restrict myself to examining the psychological meaning of locus of control, as thus measured. Actually many other more recent locus of control tests use items from this scale together with modified and similar items so that the fact there are correlations between the various measures is not really evidence for validity.

The Rotter I-E scale This scale has twenty-three items and six filler items. This suggests that, as was made clear in Chapter 2, the scale should be reliable and this is so. Thus all depends on the validity of the test, specifically its factor structure and its relationship to other well-known factors.

It is instructive to examine the original item analysis of this scale. The correlations of items with the total score are unusually small. Seventeen items have correlations of 0.29 or below, five are above 0.3 and only one is above 0.4. This does not suggest that there is a common factor accounting for the variance in these items.

Ashkanasy (1985) has reviewed much of the factor analytic work on the items in this scale and the results can be easily summarised. There are generally two factors with a large number of uninterpretable small factors. The first factor loads on items phrased in the first person, the second on items relevant to political and social institutions. All this strongly implies that there is no factor of locus of control and that the concept has arisen through psychometric ignorance – collecting a set of face valid items and calling it a test.

This negative evidence concerning the emergence of a locus of control factor arises from the study of the items themselves. It is, however, confirmed by research on the correlations and factorisations of the locus scores with other tests. Thus Lefcourt (1991) admits that the scale correlates positively with social desirability, a finding which creates little confidence in the concept of locus of control as an important personality variable.

A further study essentially demonstrates that there is little useful variance in the locus of control scale. Thus Layton (1985) correlated the test with the EPQ (see Chapter 4). He found that there were significant positive correlations with N, P and L. Given the lack of a clear factor within the items of the I-E scale, it appears that two of the important Eysenck factors and social desirability are all that is reliably measured by the test.

Conclusions It is clear that there is no common factor of locus of control. Whatever is measured by these items is largely composed of variance in other tests, especially neuroticism, psychoticism and social desirability. Since, in addition, it was argued by Lefcourt (1991) that the general locus of control factor cannot predict behaviour but that specific locus of control scales are better, there seems no reason, theoretical or psychometric, to posit a locus of control variable.

That this scale and other similar scales are widely used in social psychology demonstrates the chasm between different areas of psychology. It also demonstrates a collective madness that has overtaken various branches of psychology in which studies exist in a private world, in this case of locus of control (see Kline, 1988, for a full discussion of this problem in many different fields of psychology). Scales are used which correlate with each other mainly because their items are highly similar if not identical, and these correlations are cited as evidence of meaningfulness. Such work is hermeneutical and of no scientific value.

In brief, locus of control is not a construct that is supported by psychometrics. Indeed the contribution of psychometrics to this field is to demonstrate the inanity of the concept, a contribution, however, to which no attention has been paid.

Summary and conclusions

In this chapter I have scrutinised the findings from psychometric tests, of high repute and wide usage, which were constructed by methods other than factor analysis. The MMPI, the personality questionnaire, with the most citations in books and papers, and originally devised by criterion-keying items in the discrimination of abnormal groups, was shown to be disappointing in its substantive contribution to psychological knowledge. This monument to empiricism was useful only for screening out abnormal subjects and its recent revision, the MMPI–2, seems little improvement in this respect.

Two tests, the PRF and the MBTI, devised to measure variables in the Murray and Jungian systems respectively, were shown to be of unproven validity and, in all probability, measured little variance beyond the big five factors usually found in questionnaires. It was also shown that an interesting but little known questionnaire, the DPI, claimed to be measuring Freudian psychosexual variables, had little support for its validity although its variance did appear to be different from that in most personality questionnaires.

Finally two variables, authoritarianism and locus of control, both essentially products of psychometric testing, were scrutinised. The latter was shown to have little support conceptually or empirically and it is a concept which should be abandoned. Authoritarianism was shown, on the other hand, to be a well-founded variable and to be the social, political emanation of the obsessional personality, a personality syndrome which resembles two factors in the big five, open-mindedness and conservatism.

From this study of empirical and theoretically derived tests which were not based upon factor analysis, the only concept which has been supported is that of the authoritarian personality. This is a variable or syndrome of personality traits which must form part of the psychometric view of personality and whose theoretical implications will be discussed in Chapter 9.

Chapter 6

Personality dynamics

The psychometric view

In our opening chapter a distinction was drawn, it will be remembered, between temperamental and dynamic personality traits. The former relate to the manner of behaviour, the latter to determinants. Extraversion for example, a temperamental trait, is reflected strongly in social behaviour. As has been shown, the extravert is noisy, sociable, pushy, hungry for stimulation. This should be contrasted with dynamic traits which motivate or determine what we do. Thus, to take the same example, a person may seek out a party because she feels lonely, the dynamic trait here being the need for company or love.

As was also pointed out in the first chapter, the nature of human dynamics is a matter of considerable dispute among personality theorists, ranging from two drives, at one extreme – the Eros and Thanatos of psychoanalysis – to twenty-three or more in the theories of Murray (1938) and McDougall (1932), and even including the view of Skinnerians (Skinner, 1953) that behaviour is best regarded as controlled by reinforcers, although certain basic biological drives, such as hunger or thirst, are acceptable to them.

This theoretical confusion concerning personality dynamics suggests that it is an ideal field for the factor analytic psychometric approach to pick out the most important factors. However, there are considerable difficulties involved in the study of psychodynamics which must be discussed and examined before the results of the psychometric investigation of this field can be appreciated.

Distinction between temperamental and dynamic traits

There can be no doubt that there is a distinction between temperamental and dynamic traits. Hunger acts as a drive to seek out food and nobody would think of hunger as a personality temperamental trait. A person may be described as hungry for power or fame but again this is seen as a dynamic trait, determining behaviour.

In contrast to this, a temperamental trait such as obsessionality accounts for how people do things – neatly, precisely, in a certain order and without error. Similarly the anxious person checks train times, arrives early to ensure there is no mistake and probably books a seat. This latter example demonstrates that the distinction between temperament and dynamics is blurred. It would be reasonable to say, in this instance, that she checked her ticket because she was anxious. Thus clear temperamental traits can have a dynamic aspect.

It might be argued that anxiety is a special case since, as is discussed below, anxiety is not only a trait but is also a state (e.g. before an examination) and states or moods definitely determine behaviour. Indeed such an argument might even apply to the train whose imminent departure had produced state anxiety. This, however, will not do, if we consider the further distinction between states and traits.

Distinction between states and traits

Traits are stable characteristics unchanging over time. States are transient and may last for a very short period. Anger and fear exemplify this latter case although fear can be long lasting *(timor mortis perturbat me)* in which case it becomes a trait – timidity. The timid person varies in fearfulness (state fear increasing it from time to time). Thus, although this distinction between stable and transient, to discriminate states, is not absolute, in general it makes good sense. Most states or moods, for the difference is one of English usage rather than reflecting a psychological phenomenon, are transient. Traits are always stable or long term. It makes no sense to talk of a transient trait.

Thus to return to the distinction between dynamic and temperamental traits it has to be admitted that it is not absolute although in the majority of cases it is meaningful. Even the case of obsessionality could be seen as causing the checking and listing typical of the syndrome, although this seems to be a different sense of, or level of, causation from drives such as hunger or thirst. Despite these problems, however, it is clear that there is a useful distinction between dynamics and temperament.

It should be noted that one of the tests of temperament that was discussed in the last chapter, the PRF, measured a set of needs. This test could be conceived of as a dynamic measure since needs by definition drive behaviour. However, this test is usually regarded as a personality rather than a motivational test and, as was seen, its variance considerably overlapped two of the best known sets of temperamental factors – those of Cattell and the big five.

This introduction discusses some of the problems besetting research into the dynamics of personality. These can be briefly summarised. First there is considerable theoretical confusion concerning what are the important dynamic variables, thus making it difficult to know what to test. Secondly the distinction between dynamic and temperamental traits is not as sharp as it first appears and a further distinction between states or moods and traits has to be taken into account although even this is to some extent relative.

Factor analysis of dynamic traits

In the field of personality traits, as has been seen, the approach pioneered by Cattell has been to sample the universe of temperamental variables and to discover the most important factors by simple structure rotation. This had been previously successful in the sphere of abilities (e.g. Cattell, 1971) and this is the obvious method for clarifying human motivation.

From the introductory discussion of personality dynamics it is clear that there are two categories of motivational trait: states or moods and drives. These will be examined separately.

Factor analysis of states and moods

In addition to the general problems of research into personality dynamics which have been discussed there are some more specific, practical difficulties which create further problems for factor analysis.

States change over time. As has been argued, states are distinguished from traits by their transience. This means, as Cattell (1973) has pointed out, that any factor analysis which will reliably reveal states, as distinct from traits, must also involve time. Failure so to do renders studies of moods and states of little value, in his view, which is certainly logically impeccable. This means that regular R factor analysis involving correlations between tests, the usual approach to the field (other than by Cattell), must be treated with considerable caution because the factors could be traits or states.

Howarth (1980) is a good example of a careful R factor analysis of moods, which must be scrutinised. He based his mood adjective checklist upon a study of all previous mood scales and the R factor analysis revealed the following moods: aggression, scepticism, egotism, outgoingness, control, anxiety, cooperation, fatigue, concentration and sadness. As has been mentioned, their validity as states is dubious because they emerged from R analysis. I find it difficult to consider scepticism to be a state. Surely, in some individuals, for example Socrates or Bertrand Russell, scepticism was more than this.

Of course, workers in the field of moods who use R technique try to counter the criticism of Cattell by differentiating states and traits in terms of items. State items stress the present. 'I feel sad now' is a state item while 'I generally feel sad' measures the trait. This gives considerable face validity to mood items of this kind. Nevertheless it is not a satisfactory manoeuvre. Thus a person who is generally sad will be sad when tested.

Recently, despite these difficulties with R analysis, there has been a renewed factor analytic attack on the problem of the structure of moods by Tellegen and his colleagues. Watson and Tellegen (1985) surveyed a large number of studies of mood and reported some of their own studies. They concluded that two orthogonal factors would account for much of the variance in mood scales: positive affect and negative affect. All moods and states which are pleasant load the first factor and all unpleasant states the second. This is a powerful simplification of the field which essentially states that there are only two moods, pleasant and unpleasant.

Cooper and McConnille (1989) factored the Cattell Eight-State Questionnaire (which is discussed below) and the Tellegen scales. They showed that state anxiety was equivalent to negative affect and state exvia to positive affect. This suggests that the Tellegen scales (despite the R analysis) are equivalent to the second-order factors in the Cattell set (see below).

Cooper and McConnille (1990) also examined mood variability using again the Eight-State Questionnaire (Curran and Cattell, 1974). They found that there were considerable individual differences in mood variability. Thus subjects who varied a lot on one of the scales tended to vary a lot on all of them and vice-versa. Such results are explicable in terms of common factors underlying the Cattell scales and the Tellegen positive and negative affect factors could well be the ones.

Such variability has certain clear implications. Norms are not appropriate given the variability in scores, although norms for the actual variability itself might be possible. Single measurements of variables which fluctuate are only useful if the measurements are required at that time. Finally, if a general level of a subject's mood were to be needed several measurements are required.

The implications of all these findings from the admittedly somewhat dubious R factor analysis of states and moods will be discussed after the work of Cattell has been scrutinised.

Work of Cattell on moods and states

As has been mentioned Cattell has criticised R analyses as being unsuited to the analysis of moods. However, as was pointed out in Chapter 3, there are other forms of factor analysis than the usual analysis of the correlations between tests. These will be discussed below.

P technique

In P technique the correlations between occasions on a variety of tests for each individual are subjected to factor analysis. Thus these factors account for variance over time within an individual and must be moods or states. P factors could never be traits. However, P factor analysis has not been much used on account of a number of problems.

1 Since each individual has to be tested many times on each variable it is difficult to obtain subjects who are willing to do the tests. Even payment may not be sufficient to produce the required dedication.
2 Constant retesting is highly likely to affect the validity of tests which are not designed for such use. Subjects get bored doing the same items or remember what they put before. Sometimes semantic satiation occurs when the items are so familiar that they lose all meaning, a phenomenon which can be experienced by continuously repeating a word.
3 Time intervals. Since some moods or states last only a few minutes, time intervals to catch these would have to be impossibly short. Even testing everyday will miss some moods.
4 Sampling problems. Not only is it difficult to obtain many subjects for P studies, it is clear that those who are willing are unlikely to be a representative normal sample.
5 Case studies. In P technique the factors obtained are unique to the individual from whom they were obtained. This means that at the end of a research a collection of case studies has to be interpreted. Given all the other problems this has led Cattell (1973) and Cattell and Kline (1977) to propose two other possible methods.

dR technique

This is an R factor analysis of the differences in scores on tests of subjects on two occasions. This approach allows the use of large and representative samples and the factors, this time common to all subjects, must be moods or states because they account for variance over time. Again, as in P technique, they cannot be traits.

However, Cronbach (1984) has criticised the use of difference scores as a basis for statistical analysis on account of their large standard errors, a particularly serious problem with factor analysis. One way round this is to split the sample and to interpret only replicable factors.

Chain P technique

In this the attempt is made to combine the advantages of both methods. Thus if twenty subjects are tested on five occasions chain P technique treats the data effectively as if there were 100 testings. However, as Cattell (1973) argues this is a compromise and P technique is to be preferred.

Conclusions from the discussion of methods From this discussion of methods in the elucidation of states a number of conclusions can be drawn. The point noted previously concerning the relativity of stablility and transience, as applied to states and traits, must also be borne in mind.

1 Traits can only appear in R analysis.
2 States can appear in R, dR and P analysis.
3 Change factors can appear in dR and P analysis.

Here a new term, change factors, has been used and this must be defined. In the initial studies of moods and states reported in Cattell (1973) and Cattell and Kline (1977) a number of factors emerged from dR analyses which were similar to the traits and it made no sense to think of these as states or moods. Cattell labelled them trait-change factors. These represent the growth and decline of traits and are not motivational or moods or states. However, in all studies of states based on dR analyses or P technique it is always possible that trait-change factors may arise and they have to be distinguished from genuine states.

There are two interesting examples here – anxiety and extraversion. As has been made clear in Chapter 4, anxiety and extraversion are the two largest personality factors. In dR studies both of these emerge. Are these therefore trait-change or state factors? Anxiety is usually considered to be a state in most theories of personality and in common experience. Thus few would attempt to argue that the anxiety of dR analysis is a trait-change factor. However, exvia (Cattell's equivalent to extraversion) also appears in dR analyses. This is not normally conceptualised as a motivational or state factor so that it would, at first glance, appear to be a clear trait-change factor. However, Cattell argues that this may be a genuine state factor since, as we all know from experience, on occasions we feel sociable and on others we cannot face even a brief conversation.

Conclusions

From this discussion it is clear that, to some extent, the distinction between trait-change and state factors is subjective and that it is impossible to claim that states discovered only through R analyses are necessarily states. Factors, on the other hand, revealed through P and dR analyses must be states or trait-change factors.

Twelve Cattell state factors

From this dreadful and complex morass Cattell has argued that there are twelve state factors, although their validity and general support from other empirical work is far less than that with the personality traits. The twelve factors are: anxiety, exvia, cortertia (alertness), independence, depression (general), psychoticism, stress, fatigue, arousal, regression, and two minor depression factors.

Two tests have been developed to measure the largest of these factors, the Eight-State Questionnaire (Curran and Cattell, 1974) and the Central Trait-State Kit (Barton and Cattell, 1981) which measures the five largest second-order states and traits in the Cattell system.

Final conclusions concerning the factor analysis of moods and states

The factor analysis of moods and states has not yet reached a generally agreed structure, partly because most workers are happy with R analysis despite its problems, while only Cattell has applied P and dR analysis. Nevertheless as the study of the Tellegen scales (the best R scale) and the Eight-State Questionnaire (the best dR scale) by Cooper and McConnille (1989) showed, there is considerable overlap. State anxiety was equivalent to the negative affect scale, state extraversion to the positive affect. These authors also showed that individuals could be described along a dimension of mood variability, which supports the claim of common factors underlying separate moods.

Certainly to conceive of only two moods, pleasant and unpleasant, whose outward manifestations may vary according to circumstance, is an elegant account of moods and states but further research is needed to indicate whether this simplification is not too drastic.

It might perhaps be worthy of note, that the fact that anxiety and exvia can be seen as states (change factors) throws some doubt on the distinction between state and trait. It could be argued that certain traits such as anxiety or obsessionality, as was suggested on general principles, at the beginning of this chapter, also act as drives and this accounts for the emergence of trait-change factors.

Factor analysis of drives: motivational structure

The factor analysis of drives has proved to be even more difficult than that of states and moods. Since Cattell is about the only psychometrist who has attempted to factor drives, this section of this chapter will be largely concerned with his work, of which good accounts can be found in Cattell (1985) and Cattell and Johnson (1986).

Definition of drives

Cattell sees three aspects to drives, in the tradition of McDougall (1932). There is a tendency to attend to certain stimuli rather than others, e.g. food when hungry rather than flowers. Each drive has its own characteristic emotion and there is an impulse to some particular course of action. Clearly, therefore, to understand motivated behaviour in these terms it is necessary to elucidate the structure of drives which underlies it.

Drives can be looked at in another way: as Cattell (1957, 1985) argues, attitudes reflect drives because the strength of an attitude reflects the strength of an impulse to action in response to a stimulus. It is on these grounds that Cattell further argues that the factor analysis of attitudes will reveal drives. This conceptualisation of drives also implicates, it should be noted, interests. These also must be held to be accounted for by drives. This is certainly true incidentally in psychoanalytic theory where, for example, interest in surgery reflects sublimated aggression and in art, sublimated anal erotism (Fenichel, 1945). Hence the factor analysis and measurement of interest ought to reveal motivational factors.

Measurement of interests

At this point a brief paragraph on the measurement of interests is required. This is because there is a considerable number of interest tests which have been largely developed for practical occupational psychology to aid in selection. and career development, a use of psychometrics which is discussed in Chapter 8 of this book. However, such tests have revealed nothing concerning the nature of human motivation because they were constructed not by factor analysis which might have revealed underlying determining factors, but, in the main, by criterion-keyed methods which, as was shown in Chapter 2, yield variables of unknown psychological meaning. I shall briefly mention these and other non-factor analytic tests of motivation at the end of this chapter but essentially they are unable to yield useful information about dynamic structure.

Strength of interest

There is one further aspect to interests which needs to be measured. This is strength of interest. It is obvious from experience that not only do interests differ but so also does strength of interest. Cattell and Child (1975) list from a search of the literature relating to expressions of attitude and interest sixty-eight indices and report the results of a number of simple structure factor analyses. Such tests as these are, in the categories adopted in Chapter 2, objective tests. These strength of interest factors are set out below:

Alpha – 'conscious id' This is the component related to the satisfaction of personal desires even when this is unwise. Politicians caught in sexual or financial scandals exemplify the working of this component.

Beta – realised integrated interest This is the ego component of attitudes, the rational aspect, the only part tested by standard attitude questionnaires.

Gamma – 'superego' The moral component of interests, the aspect of interest revealed in the pseudo-interests of the middle classes in the arts.

Delta This is a physiological component to interest reflected in the thrilling sensations – spine tingling – to certain stimuli.

Epsilon This seems to be a conflict factor, perhaps related to depression.

There were two further unidentified primary factors.

At the second-order, three factors emerged:

Integrated component This loads on beta and gamma and reflects reality and information-based experience – the rational aspect of attitudes and interest.

Unintegrated component This loads on alpha, delta and epsilon and thus reflects aspects of interests below the level of awareness.

There was a third unidentified component.

As has been argued by Kline (1981) these strength of interest factors, especially at the second-order, fit a general psychoanalytic model of interests in that their strength reflects conscious and unconscious components.

These findings have important implications for the measurement and understanding of attitudes, interests and motivation. Thus it is clear that all attitude measurement must involve these factors, certainly the two main second-orders. As has been mentioned, the standard attitude questionnaire which contains simple face-valid items relevant to the interest or attitude cannot do this. Such scales are solely concerned with the integrated, rational component. This almost certainly accounts for the weak predictive power of standard attitude scales. Cattell (Cattell, Horn and Sweney, 1970) has developed the Motivational Analysis Test to measure the most important drives as well as interest strength and this will be discussed later in this chapter.

It must be pointed out, however, that beyond the boundaries of Cattell and his colleagues, this factor analytic approach to attitudes and motivation is not only not accepted, it is virtually unknown. This is particularly unfortunate since it means that the factors have been little explored so that there is little external evidence to support them.

In brief these strength of interest factors still require further research before they could be accepted as definitive accounts of the attitude strength. However, they represent psychometric hypotheses which deserve proper exploration.

The structure of drives

The same objective tests, based on indices and expressions of interest, can also be used to tap drives and this has been done by Cattell and his colleagues and reported in Cattell and Child (1975) and Cattell (1985).

Although the work of Cattell is empirical, there were models and theories broadly underlying the selection of tests in the first place. A truly atheoretical collection of data is impossible. These theories were broadly those of McDougall (1932), Murray (1938) and Freud (1933), who have in common the notion that drives are reflected in interests and that various behaviours can be traced back to certain goals and that one behaviour may relate to several goals. For example, an interest in cars may reflect various goals: to arouse envy, to feel powerful, to attract women or men, to exhibit wealth.

This raises yet another aspect of the structure of drives. In analysing the goals of any behaviour, it is often found that the goals are ordered, until ultimately a final goal is reached. Examples of these are to get food, to obtain warmth, to enjoy sexual activity. These are considered by Cattell and most other theorists to be basic biological drives, which can be observed in many other organisms, especially mammals. In Cattell's neology these basic biological drives are ergs. These are contrasted with sentiments which are culturally moulded drives, uniquely human.

As has been mentioned, Cattell and his colleagues have subjected objective tests which, from studies of the psychology of motivation, would appear to reflect drives, to simple structure factor analyses and the most recent list of ergs and sentiments is set out below. Further details of these factors may be found in Sweney *et al.* (1986) and Gorsuch (1986).

A Replicated ergs:
Food-seeking; escape to security; mating; self-assertion; gregariousness; narcissism; parental pity; pugnacity; exploration; acquisitiveness.

B Other ergs (of uncertain identification):
Appeal; constructiveness; rest-seeking; self-abasement; and (even less clearly defined) laughter and disgust.

C Well-defined sentiments:
Career; self-sentiment; home-parental; sports and games; mechanical; partner; religious; superego.

I shall discuss the ergs first. As was the case with the strength of interest factors, these drive factors have been little investigated except by Cattell and colleagues which inevitably means that there is still insufficient evidence to establish their validity. Far more research than is reported in Cattell (1985) or by Sweney *et al.* (1986) is required before it is possible to regard these as established motivational factors. Again as was the case with the strength of interest factors this is particularly unfortunate, since this list of ergs, if shown to be correct, would constitute an important contribution from psychometrics to personality research. This is because it demonstrates that there are more drives than postulated by Freud and less than the vast lists of Murray and McDougall. In other words, psychometric measurement has been able to improve on the speculations of even the best theorists. Thus it is essential that efforts are made to validate and explicate these factors.

As regards the list of sentiments, the position is different. Although these are the best-defined sentiments, Gorsuch (1986) admits that this is not a complete or definitive list. Nevertheless, as can be seen, they do represent the most obviously important interests and drives in Western culture. These are of little theoretical psychological interest but represent activities which happen to be important in that culture. Indeed these sentiments are not dissimilar to the variables of interest tests completed by item analyses of face-valid items derived from common-sense knowledge of human interests and activities, tests which will be discussed at the end of the chapter.

As was pointed out above, Cattell has developed one objective motivation test, the MAT (Cattell, Horn and Sweney, 1970), based upon his factor analytic studies of motivation, and this will be described. I shall further examine a factor analytic measure of interests, designed specifically for occupational psychology, the Vocational Interest Measure, the VIM (Sweney and Cattell, 1980).

The Motivational Analysis Test

The MAT (Cattell, Horn and Sweney, 1970) is one of the few objective tests which has been published as a test for general use. This measures the ten best-established motivational factors – five ergs and five sentiments. These are: mating, assertiveness, fear, narcissism and pugnacity (the ergs); self-sentiment, superego or conscience, career, partner and parental home (the sentiments). In addition the integrated and unintegrated components of interest strength are measured.

There are four kinds of objective test in the MAT:

1 Questionnaire items in which subjects have to indicate what is the better use of a given amount of time, money or some other commodity.
2 Estimates of feelings have to be given on a four-point scale. For example, 'What percent of adults are happy to give to charity?'

Both these tests measure the unintegrated component of drives and it should be noted that, although they are of the questionnaire form, they are objective because the purpose of the items is hidden from subjects including most psychologists.

3 Paired words in which subjects have to indicate which of a pair of words goes better with a key word.
4 Information. This is a knowledge test, claimed by Cattell and Child (1975) to measure interests because people know most about what they are interested in.

Both these tests measure the integrated, rational component of strength of interest.

Reliability and validity of the MAT There is little doubt that the

Cattellian approach to the measurement of motivation is brilliant in conception. However, its instantiation in the MAT is not satisfactory. In the handbook to the test the scales are of low reliability, the median alpha being only 0.45.

Kline and Grindley (1974) showed, in a twenty-eight-day case study where a subject completed a diary and the MAT every day, that fluctuations in ergs and sentiments corresponded to diary events in a striking manner. This led us to investigate the validity of the test with more psychometric rigour.

To this end Cooper and Kline (1982) carried out an oblique simple structure rotation of the 16PF and MAT but only eight factors emerged and none of these was in accord with expectation. Item analyses also showed that the scales were not homogeneous, items not fitting the scales of which they were a part. From this study it must be concluded that the MAT is not a valid test, at least in Great Britain, although it certainly deserves much further research and development.

The Vocational Interest Measure, VIM (Sweney and Cattell, 1980)

This, like the MAT, is an objective, factor analytic test, but one specifically designed to measure occupational interests and to be useful for occupational psychology.

Variables measured Two ergs: protectiveness and rest-seeking. Eight sentiments: career, mechanical interests, clerical work interests, scientific work interests, aesthetic-dramatic interests, business-economic interests, sports interests and nature-outdoor interests.

Although first developed in 1980, this was an experimental version of the test and, as the article by Sweney *et al.* (1986) shows, at present it still requires external validation against success at relevant occupations. Without this it cannot be used for anything but research into its own validity and into the viability of Cattell's factor analytic approach to motivation.

The interest of this test lies in the fact that it is a part of a factor analytic exploration of motivation, although it is likely that the variables which the VIM attempts to measure are of less psychological importance than those in the MAT, because these seem to be fundamental aspects of the human organism (ergs) and of human culture. The VIM variables, on the other hand, seem applicable only to a particular set of jobs in Western society and although the test may prove valuable in the practice of occupational psychology it seems unlikely to throw much light on motivation in general.

Before completing this chapter by drawing out substantive conclusions from the psychometric study of personality, brief mention must be made of motivation and interest tests which were not derived from factor analysis.

Two of the most widely used American tests, the Strong Vocational Interest Blank (Strong *et al.*, 1971) and its modern form the Strong-Campbell Interest Inventory (Strong and Campbell, 1974), and the various forms of the Kuder Tests (Kuder, 1970a, 1970b), for a variety of reasons can make no strong contribution to the psychometry of motivation. Thus the Strong tests were developed by criterion-keying and items were selected which could discriminate one occupational group from another. Such scales, as has been argued in Chapter 2, have no psychological meaning so that the results are only useful if good discriminations can be made between groups. In fact the discrimination is little better than expressed interest.

The Kuder Occupational Interest Survey (Kuder, 1970b) in which the items were selected if endorsed by an occupational group, an alternative form of criterion-keying, again has scales which lack psychological meaning. Furthermore, this method ensures that many individuals seem suited to a variety of occupations, which is useful for discussion and counselling but of little practical value in selection. Another form of this test, the Kuder General Interest Survey (Kuder, 1970a), is ipsatively scored which makes comparison between the scores of individuals meaningless. While this test may be useful for discussion in occupational counselling it cannot make any contribution to a knowledge of motivation.

The last test which I shall discuss is the Vocational Preference Inventory, the VPI, constructed by Holland (1985a) and the measuring instrument developed as part of his theory of vocational choice (Holland, 1985b). This test, in as much as it is part of a theory, is of potentially considerable psychological interest if the validity of either test or theory could be supported.

Description of the VPI

The items of this test consist of occupational titles to which subjects indicate like or dislike. These form nine interest scales: realistic, investigative, artistic, social, enterprising, conventional, self-control, masculinity–femininity and status. The internal consistencies of these scales are generally high although three are only around 0.5.

Over more than thirty years Holland has developed his theory of occupational choice and the results of more than 400 investigations with the VPI can be called upon as evidence. Nevertheless, despite this huge array of results, the research can be summarised.

Holland (1985a, 1985b) has shown that there is a moderate correlation between his personality types as defined by the scales and job choice. This supports Holland's occupational theory which claims that personality types seek out jobs suited to them. The predictive and concurrent validity of the VPI scales relative to job choice is at least as good as that of the Strong and Kuder tests.

Holland also regards these scales as measures of personality and has correlated them with the main personality test scales discussed in Chapters 4 and 5. There are numerous moderate correlations which make reasonable psychological sense. Thus, for example, the VPI enterprising scale correlated with Cattell's A, sociability; E, dominance; F, enthusiasm; and H, adventurousness. All this suggests that the VPI may be measuring nothing more than the ubiquitous big five factors or even more simply the two largest of these, extraversion and neuroticism. This means, of course, that strictly the VPI is a temperamental rather than a dynamic scale.

To some extent this is supported by the study by Costa *et al.* (1984) with the NEO inventory when one scale correlated with neuroticism, two with extraversion and three with openness. An ongoing study in which the 16PF and the VPI were subjected to oblique, simple structure factor analysis strongly suggests that two factors can explain the VPI variance – neuroticism and extraversion – and that these are more associated with career choice among adolescents than are the simple VPI scales (Parker and Kline, 1992).

Conclusions concerning the VPI This test which is tied to the theory of Holland concerning occupational choice is probably no worse than many others at predicting choice. However, this is done with simple face-valid items and is of little psychological interest. More interesting is the fact that these scales probably together measure anxiety or neuroticism and extraversion and are not independent. It is clear no powerful motivational theory could depend on the VPI.

Final conclusions

From this chapter it is quite clear that factor analysis has not so far led to considerable substantive conclusions. This is because the majority of users of motivational and interest tests are applied psychologists who are not concerned with theoretical issues such as the number of drives or the nature of drive strength. All they require is an effective test for selection and counselling. Such tests can be easily made by techniques which do not lead on to theoretical insights.

The only factor analytic attempt of any substance in the motivational field is that of Cattell but, as has been seen, there are profound difficulties in establishing mood or state factors (where R analysis is insufficient) as well as other dynamic factors.

However, as a result of the reluctance of practical occupational psychologists to use these factored tests, the factors emerging from the Cattell work have not been validated in the field so that there is insufficient external evidence relevant to their psychological meaning. Furthermore, factored studies of the tests do not suggest that they are measuring the variables claimed for them.

In brief, this is a field in which psychometrics has not yet made a substantive contribution, except perhaps in the notion of only two state factors – positive and negative affect, although even here these factors require further validation. However, the methods and approaches, P and dR analyses and the validation of emerging factors, are all ready for use and all that is needed is technically adequate research.

Chapter 7

Heritability of personality

The question of the heritability of personality is one of the most fundamental in the psychology of personality. This is because any psychological theory must take into account the heritability of the variables with which it is concerned. Thus if, for example, the heritability of anxiety were zero it is clear that its status would be entirely dependent on environmental factors and any theory must be able to state what these are and how they affect anxiety. Similarly if environmental effects are zero, as in the case of eye colour, to postulate environmental influences must be wrong. Clearly then, to determine the heritability of personality variables is essential for any adequate theory of personality and for a good understanding of the field.

In addition, there are further powerful arguments from the study of the heritability of personality which can be brought to bear on the problems of understanding personality. The first relates to already extant theories of personality which are either refuted or supported by the findings. Thus if it turns out that much of the variance of personality is determined by genetic factors, theories in the psychoanalytic tradition, in which great emphasis is placed on the importance of child-rearing, are in some difficulty.

The second argument is only relevant to the psychometric approach to personality but is of critical importance to the interpretation of the personality factors which have been discussed in the last three chapters. As was made clear in our discussions in earlier chapters of test validity and of factor analysis, a major problem in any psychometric factor analytic study is the identification of the factors or their validity. Normally they are interpreted from their factor loadings and by external validation, although this latter is often difficult to establish in the case of personality factors.

Establishing the heritability of personality factors is a particularly useful form of external validation because if it turns out that a factor has considerable genetic determination, a major criticism of factor analytic personality variables is, at a stroke, removed. This criticism is the always logically possible argument (in the case of personality questionnaires) that the factors are no more than bloated specifics, collections of items that are essentially paraphrases of each other. It makes no sense that a putative bloated specific has a considerable portion of its variance determined by hereditary factors, so that, if it thus turns out, the factor cannot be specific. Factors whose variance is determined to any considerable extent (and this will be precisely defined later in this chapter) by hereditary factors cannot be any kind of statistical artifact and must be of some psychological significance.

In brief, determining the heritability of personality variables is of considerable theoretical interest in the study of personality, and is perhaps especially important to the psychometric factor analytic view of personality.

Biometric analysis

In this chapter I shall examine the findings from the biometric analysis of personality. Biometric analysis involves the study of the sources of variance within populations with reference to genetic and environmental components. Several important points about biometric analyses should be noted at the outset before a more detailed description and rationale of the procedures is given.

Within populations This is a highly significant phrase. If it is found, for example, that 40 per cent of the variance of a particular personality trait is determined by genetic factors it does not mean that 40 per cent of that trait in any individual is determined genetically and the rest by her environment. These figures refer to sources of variation within a population.

It is also important to note that the heritability ratios computed for one population are not necessarily the same for another. Thus in a population, for example, where environmental factors were of low variance (perhaps where there were strict rules of child rearing), hereditary factors would be relatively of greater significance in determining individual differences.

Finally at this juncture, it is important to remember that if within a population a trait has a considerable genetic determination, it does not follow that differences in that trait between two populations must be so determined, as Plomin (1986) has demonstrated.

Biometric methods

Although these methods are algebraically complex, Fulker (1979) has provided a brilliant, simplified version which I set out below.

P = G + E where P is the phenotypic variance (the observed variance, e.g. the scores on a test), G is the variance determined genetically and E is the variance environmentally determined. By the use of variances in this model it is possible to separate out G and E from the variances and covariances of groups of individuals such as twins.

The analysis of variance of twin pairs partitions the variance into two sources: between and within pairs. The more pairs resemble each other, the greater the between pairs variance will be compared with the within pairs variance. Indeed, the ratio of (B-W)/(B+W) yields the intra-class correlation showing how similar pairs of twins are. From these variances and correlations, the genetic and environmental components can be derived.

E, the environmental variance, can be broken down into two parts: the common or shared environment (CE) reflecting the experiences of home life which are common to members of a family and the specific environment (SE) or unshared aspects of experience. The biometric equation can then be written:

P = G + CE + SE.

With this model a number of deductions can be made.

The correlation (r) reflects the variance of all shared influences.

a Identical (MZ) twins. r = G + CE;
b Non-identical twins. r + ½G + CE (these having half their genes in common).

From these assumptions the following estimates can be made:

G = twice the difference between the two correlations;
CE = the difference between the MZ correlation and the estimate of G;
SE = 100 – G + CE.

This is the basic reasoning behind the biometric approach to the analysis of the genetic and environmental determinants of the variance of any trait within a population. It should be noted that this is the most simple additive model. However, it is possible to increase its complexity and its accuracy by using the intra-class correlations derived from relatives other than twins, and allowing for dominance and assortative mating for example, where this occurs, as it does in the case of intelligence where more intelligent individuals tend to choose more intelligent partners (and have more intelligent children).

From this discussion it can be seen that biometric analyses determine the sources of variation of traits within populations by examining the variances and covariances among individuals of all degrees of relatedness reared apart and together. Relatives reared apart are a particularly valuable group because this sets CE in the equations at zero.

As Jinks and Fulker (1970) argue, the fact that these biometrical methods were developed for agricultural and biological use is no reason for supposing that they would not work in the human case. All that is required for these methods are trait measures and the requisite samples of relatives. This is what makes biometric methods well suited to the psychometric approach to personality since this involves personality tests yielding numerical data.

From our description of biometric methods it is clear that twin studies are important to them. However, on their own, although they have been traditionally used in investigations of the influence of heredity, especially of intelligence, they are inadequate for a number of reasons. First, studies of identical (monozygotic) twins reared apart are likely to underestimate the contribution of genetic factors. This is because there are sources of discordance among identical twins which, although neither environmental nor genetic in the ordinary sense of the words, would be classified as environmental in twin studies where all differences must be so attributed. These special factors which have been described by Darlington (1970) include nuclear differences which arise by gene mutation or by chromosomal loss or gain when the zygote splits; cytoplasmic differences which are brought about by deleterious genes acting differentially on the two organisms; embryological differences created by errors arising in a late splitting and what is perhaps the most common: nutritional differences due to unequal placentation. This last is probably highly important in the light of recent research which shows that early nutrition (profoundly affected by placental size) has considerable physical effects in twins (Bryan, 1992).

There are further problems with twin studies. For example, the number of twins reared apart is obviously small and they may not be a representative sample of identical twins, thus making generalisations to normally reared twins difficult. This is an extension of the problem of whether it is safe to extrapolate from twins to singletons. The twin method assumes that genetic and environmental influences are uncorrelated and that they combine additively without interaction. This assumption may be difficult since it is likely that the environment of intelligent individuals, for example, is somewhat different from that of the less intelligent. Intelligent children respond differently than the less intelligent and provoke different responses. Finally, the twin method can be criticised on the grounds that twins are treated more alike than are singletons, especially MZ twins, thus apparently increasing genetic determinants of similarity. However, Loehlin and Nichols (1976) have shown that the personality scores of pairs of twins treated similarly were no more alike than the scores of twins not so treated, although the work of Rose *et al.* (1988), which is discussed below, indicates that increased social contact may enhance similarity.

However, in contrast to working with simple differences between twins, in biometric methods, as has been shown, the total variance is broken down into the between families and within families variance. In addition, the contribution of the interaction of the genetic and environmental variance, as well as the correlation between them, can be taken into account. Indeed, as Jinks and Fulker (1970) argue, one of the great advantages of biometric analyses is that it is possible to test different genetic models. There is no need to postulate a simple linear model but the effects of correlated genetic and environmental factors and of interactions can be investigated as well as the influence of gene dominance and assortative mating.

It seems difficult to attack this biometric approach to the investigation of genetic factors in personality particularly where the studies use the more complex models discussed above, since in the fields of biology and agriculture it has proved highly valuable. However, Feldman and Lewontin (1975) have argued that analysis of variance cannot separate variation which results from environmental fluctuation from that due to genetic segregation. However, it appears that these arguments do not apply to the biometric analyses discussed by Jinks and Fulker (1970) and the subject of this chapter. Thus Feldman and Lewontin (1975) claim, and this is one of their strongest objections, that broad heritability, total genetic variance, is not a useful statistic in human population genetics. What is important, they argue, is the narrow heritability, the proportion of variance due to additive genetic variance. However, in the biometric analyses in this chapter, both broad and narrow heritability can be computed, and it is clear that these criticisms are not pertinent to these procedures.

One further possible objection remains to be discussed. Uninformed criticism of the findings of biometric analyses in terms of variance attributed to genetic or environmental factors has often been concerned with the environmental findings. Such critics argue that since measuring the environment is so difficult, partly due to the fact that it is not an objective but a subjective phenomenon, and indeed there are no well-accepted measures of environmental variables, then the results must be flawed; poor measurement leading to inevitable error. This however is mistaken, since estimates of the environmental component of population variance are derived by including in them what cannot be attributed to genetic factors. This is clear from the equations at the beginning of this chapter.

The MAVA method

This is the method used by Cattell to compute the heritabilities of the factors in his system, factors which have been described in earlier chapters of this book. I shall describe it briefly because some results derived from it will be discussed later in this chapter. Cattell (1982) in a detailed account of his work on the inheritance of personality and ability sets out the complex algebra of the MAVA (multiple analysis of variance) method for computing the heritability of traits. This MAVA method deals with four sources of variance: variability among siblings due to within family genetic variance; variance within the family due to environmental influences; variance between families due to genetic influences and variance between families due to environmental differences. In addition, covariances and interaction terms can be added. To solve these equations data are needed from twins, identical and non-identical, siblings and individuals with other degrees of relationship reared up together and apart.

I shall not describe the MAVA method in more detail because, although it is undoubtedly superlative, Jinks and Fulker (1970) indeed describe it as a brilliant one-man attempt to develop a statistics of genetic biometrics, it has certain difficulties which the more usual biometric analyses described earlier have overcome. One difficulty with MAVA is that a subjective decision has to be made as to whether interaction terms are included in the equations or not. This is because to include all possibilities would involve impossibly large and usually unobtainable samples. Furthermore there are some doubts about the logic of the algebra of MAVA, although this is a topic which cannot be dealt with here. Given these problems, it seems more sensible to deal with the standard biometrical analyses rather than the more idiosyncratic methods of Cattell. However, in most cases, MAVA and the standard procedures are in good agreement where both have been used as in the case of intelligence (see Cattell, 1982). Thus where only MAVA has been used I shall treat the results as worthy of brief discussion although some caution needs to be shown on account of the problems which have been raised above.

Findings from the biometrical analyses of personality

In the remainder of the chapter I shall discuss the heritability ratios and the models of genetic and environmental variance which have been determined for the personality factors shown to be important in the last three chapters of this book. As has been indicated, the results to be discussed were obtained either from orthodox biometric analysis of personality test scores or from the MAVA method in the case of Cattell's factors.

Much of this discussion will turn on the heritability of the Eysenck factors because, as has been seen, these are three factors which account for much of the variance within personality questionnaires and whose psychological meaning is known. For this purpose there are two excellent sources of information – Eaves *et al.* (1989) and Eysenck (1990) – and readers should consult these for further details. As this is written (June, 1992) an excellent new and clearly written book is about to appear (Loehlin, 1992) which gives a fine exposition of biometric approaches and summarises much of the evidence for personality tests.

As Eysenck (1990) points out, there are six modern investigations of the genetics of personality, which employ biometric analyses and these form the basis of the summary reported below. These are:

1 Work on the EPQ with 500 pairs of MZ and DZ twins, fully reported in Eaves *et al.* (1989).
2 Research by Loehlin and Nichols (1976) on 8,660 sets of twins in the USA. Unfortunately they used the CPI which is a criterion-keyed test of dubious validity (see Kline, 1992a) although they attempted to extract face-valid measures of E and N from it.
3 An Australian study by Martin and Jardine (1986) using 4,000 pairs of twins and the EPQ plus other attitude and personality measures.
4 A Swedish study with nearly 13,000 pairs of twins and a short form of the EPI, a precursor of the EPQ, measuring E and N (Floderus-Myrhed *et al.*, 1980).
5 American studies, e.g. Tellegen *et al.* (1988) on twins reared apart and together. However, these authors used a test of personality of unknown validity, thus making the results difficult to interpret.
6 More than 7,000 pairs of adult twins studied by Rose *et al.* (1988) in Finland.

The main results are as follows, although it should be noted that these biometric analyses are based upon twins.

A The between family environmental variance, the variance from the shared environment, is a trivial component of personality variance. This is a finding which has been replicated in almost all studies (other than Rose *et al.*, 1988) and is based on data from 106 pairs of identical twins reared apart and more than 5,000 pairs of identical twins reared together.

This is an astonishing finding which is contrary to almost all theories of personality which stress the importance of the family environment. Factors such as the education and social class of the family, their attitudes and values, even to child rearing, have no effect on personality. What is important in the environmental determinants of personality are the unique experiences of each individual. Note, however, that this may include the particular way in which a mother responds to each of her children, thus not ruling out psychoanalytic theories, but casting considerable doubt on more socially oriented approaches. As Eysenck (1990) argues, earlier work (e.g. Shields, 1962) which had shown that twins separated earlier were more alike than those separated later, is consonant with this position although it is a curious finding which requires further explanation.

However, the one contradictory investigation concerning the negligible impact of the shared environment (Rose *et al.*, 1988) requires some further comment. These authors found that the longer twins were together the more alike they were, although it could be the case that similarity caused twins to increase their social contact, rather than the other way round. These authors attribute the failure of most statistical studies to find differences arising from the shared environment to errors: the limited statistical power with which twin samples test environmental sources of variance; the unreliability of personality measures and the allocation of error variance to the unshared environment; the tendency for inferences about sources of environmental variation to be based on global estimates rather than direct measurement and the misleading estimates of shared environment arising from the relation of MZ and DZ correlations, misleading on account of differences in social contact between the two types of twins.

This work of Rose *et al.* (1988) cannot be held to refute all the other findings, but clearly some caution should be shown in making extravagant claims that all previous personality theories are absolutely wrong. In this study, increased social contact was related to greater similarity within pairs of twins.

B Personality variance appears to have a considerable genetic component on all the traits which have been analysed. At present in all the populations tested this is around 50 per cent. However, if the unreliability of the measures were taken into account, this could rise to 60 per cent. What is particularly interesting here is not only that fundamental personality dimensions, such as E, N and P, have these large genetic components but so too do attitude scales of the kind which most sociologists would regard as simply the results of social factors. Authoritarian and conservative attitudes are examples of these. The work of Eaves *et al.* (1989) is particularly interesting here because even at the item level strong genetic determination can be shown, as for example the following items:

> Sex crimes, such as rape and attacks on children, deserve more than mere imprisonment: such criminals ought to be flogged or worse.
>
> Men and women have the right to find out whether they are suited sexually before marriage.
>
> The average man can lead a good enough life without religion.

Once again, as was the case with the finding that the shared environment was of trivial importance, the fact that such basic social attitudes are considerably genetically determined is surprising, at the very least.

C For N the data support an additive genetic model whereas for E the pattern is different. It follows a competition model in which a sociable child gets the friends and leaves the books for her introverted sibling (Eaves *et al.*, 1989).

D In the large sample studies (Sweden and Australia) there appear to be differences between the sexes. Thus for N there are genetic effects that are specific to males and females. However, it must be remembered that with large samples psychologically unimportant differences may be statistically significant.

E Eysenck (1990) argues that there is evidence that different genes operate at different stages of development (young and old). However, during adult life the same genes seem to be operating (Eaves *et al.*, 1989).

F As regards assortative mating, it does not occur with respect to E and N and only to a slight extent in the case of P. In this, these personality variables are completely different from intelligence where assortative mating is important in explaining phenotypic variance.

These are the main findings from the large-scale studies of twins which were cited above. Of these the two most striking are the importance of genetic determinants in the variance of the main personality factors E, N and P and the lack of impact of the shared environment.

It should be pointed out that in a recent publication Loehlin (1992) has summarised the biometric studies carried out with the big five factors. These all show considerable genetic determination, similar to that discussed for the EPQ and again the shared environment has little effect on the variance.

There are other important issues in the biometric analysis of personality which must now be scrutinised. First, as was made clear at the beginning of this section, these results were concerned with P, E and N although brief mention was made of the social attitude findings of Eaves *et al.* (1989) and the fact that the big five factors appeared to be similar, in respect of genetic and environmental determination, to E, P and N. This introduces the important question as to what extent other personality variables are genetically determined.

In general, studies of other personality factors have yielded similar results, although there are differences between factors. One of the best sources for this is Cattell (1982) in which the Cattell personality factors were subjected to biometric analyses using his own MAVA method. This shows an overall heritability for all traits of 0.38. However, it must be realised that the Cattell factors are not highly reliable and this error boosts the environmental component. Furthermore methods, such as MAVA, which use other relatives (not only twins) tend to yield lower heritability ratios.

Conclusions

From these studies it must be concluded that there is a considerable genetic determination of the population variance in personality and even social attitudes and that the shared environment has little effect. What matters in personality in respect of environmental determinants appears to be the unique experiences of each person. Certainly theories which posit as important in personality development variables which discriminate families such as attitudes, social class and education, are unlikely to be correct.

Chapter 8

Personality testing in applied psychology

In this chapter I shall discuss the use of personality tests in applied psychology. I have chosen to examine how personality tests are applied because these applications are the most obvious fruits of the psychometric approach to personality, although, as will become clear, there is more to the contribution to applied psychology from psychometric studies of personality than good personality tests. The term 'applied psychology' refers here to three areas in which the results of psychometric studies of personality and personality tests are used: educational, clinical and occupational psychology, each of which will be scrutinised separately although, in fact, as shall be seen, there is some degree of overlap.

Occupational psychology

Occupational psychology is concerned with the psychological problems involved in work. These include selection and appraisal of workers, ensuring that workers are as efficient as possible, often done by designing machines and organising work to be in accord with human psychology, dealing with conflicts and disputes at work and attempting to ensure that personnel are not discontented: stress reduction as it is sometimes called. As might be expected from this description of occupational psychology, the major contribution from personality testing has been to personnel selection especially and to appraisal. It is, therefore, with these two aspects of occupational psychology that this section of the chapter will be concerned.

Personality tests in personnel selection

Psychometric testing (including also tests of ability) in personnel selection has become big business, both in Great Britain and America, where enormous numbers of psychological tests are administered for all kinds of occupations. In this section I shall deal with the rationale and methods rather than the detailed results which must be sought in more specialised books (see Herriot, 1989; Kline, 1992b) and journals, although the main findings, which are relatively clear, will be scrutinised.

The rationale of personality testing in personnel work

There is an assumption underlying the use of personality tests in job selection that for any job there is an ideal specification of psychological characteristics for it. Indeed this is an assumption of what might be called the psychometric model of human behaviour, namely that a person's behaviour can be predicted if we have a full description of her psychological traits. This underlies the work of Cattell (1957) who has produced a set of specification equations for jobs (Cattell, Eber and Tatsuoko, 1970), as will be discussed below.

It will be obvious that, with such an assumption, the task of personnel selection becomes one of fitting people to the correct job. To such a task there are two aspects: measuring people and measuring jobs. Obviously personality testing is an integral part of the first of these aspects – measuring people.

Evidence of this assumption that personality characteristics play an important part in determining behaviour is well founded, particularly as regards achievement and enjoyment at work. It arises from two sources. First everyday observation strongly suggests that personality traits are important in job success and satisfaction. Librarians, especially those concerned with cataloguing, must be orderly and like a quiet life, quite different it would appear from the work of a publican or circus ring-master. Similarly SAS officers would need somewhat different characteristics, one would have thought, from child-care workers. These observations are supported by the mass of empirical research which has been carried out over the years by occupational psychologists. Huge bodies of data exist which demonstrate that such intuitive observations are correct. There are considerable differences in personality traits between the holders of different jobs and personality characteristics do correlate with job success, as is documented in Herriot (1989), Kline (1992b) and Cook (1988).

A few examples from the 16PF test (Cattell, Eber and Tatsuoko, 1970) will illustrate this point. Artists are low on G (conscientious) and high on M (unconventional); technical personnel are high on B (intelligence) and low on I (tough-minded); social workers are high on A (warm) and low on L (trusting); scientists are low on A (cold), high on B (intelligence), and low on G and O (conscientiousness and guilt). These are sufficient to indicate that personality tests are useful in personnel work. Incidentally, the low conscientiousness and guilt scores of scientists are noteworthy in the light of the need for scientists of scrupulous honesty of reporting.

Personality tests can be used in personnel selection in three ways.

Matching In this method the scores of an applicant on a personality test are matched with the scores of the occupants of the relevant position. The subject whose scores match best is the one selected. In a good selection procedure, scores on ability tests would also be included in the profile of scores to be matched but personality tests are highly useful because, as has been seen, they usually provide several scales. Cattell, Eber and Tatsuoko (1970) have a set of profiles on the 16PF for various occupations to which each applicant can be statistically matched.

There are several problems with the matching method which need to be noted.

Sampling It is essential that the sample groups to which the applicants are matched are representative of the occupations. If they are not error is inevitable. This means the normative groups should be large and well sampled.

Difficulty of matching groups Since there are so many different jobs in many cases there will be no precisely similar group to which the subjects can be matched. In this case it is possible to match with the nearest group, but caution must be shown in interpreting the results, for obvious reasons. A similar point arises in the case of tests with American occupational group norms. Even where the name of the occupation is the same it is doubtful if the jobs require the same psychological characteristics, so that any matching might be misleading. Indeed, in many cases, tests have so few norms that the matching method cannot be used

In-house norms For the reasons above, personnel selectors in large organisations prefer to match applicants to in-house norms. This is efficient providing that such norms are derived from substantial samples. This, of course, is not possible in small firms.

Changing job demands The demands of jobs, hence also the requisite psychological characteristics, change over time, as for example when computers begin to be used. Thus profiles for matching need to be updated regularly.

The logic of matching A more fundamental difficulty arises when the logic of matching profiles is examined. Clearly it assumes an ideal world where everyone is in the job which is best suited to them. Since this is far from the case given the phenomenon of nepotism and the inefficiency of much job selection, how can the matching method be justified?

Despite these problems the vast majority of job holders are reasonably efficient and can tolerate their jobs. If this were not the case firms would fail. Thus it is still true that a particular occupational group is far more likely to possess the psychological characteristics necessary for that occupation than is any other group. This is sufficient justification.

Conclusions

From this it is clear that where good norms exist the matching method is a useful procedure. However, in practice norms may be weak or non-existent. Obviously in the latter instance the method cannot be used and in the former modifications have to be made. Usually, in this instance in practice, it makes sense to note the high and low scores of the relevant group and look for similar peaks and troughs in the subjects. This makes for less discriminating selection, for there may be many such candidates who must then be further discriminated on other criteria. However, statistically precise profile matching is nonsensical unless the profiles are derived from representative and large groups of relevant workers.

The regression method In this method regression equations, multiple correlations, are computed between the personality test scores and job success. These multiple correlations yield the overall correlation of the scores with success at the job and beta weights which indicate the importance of each score in the correlation. For example, if we were to select lawyers by the regression method, the scores on each scale are multiplied by the beta weights and the total of the weighted scores indicates suitability for the post. The applicant with the highest weighted total is the best suited. The higher the multiple correlation the greater reliance one can place on the weighted total. There are several important points to be noted about this regression method.

Sampling Clearly the samples on which the multiple correlations were derived must be large and representative. Furthermore since beta weights have large standard errors it is important that these weights have been replicated in more than one study. However, correcting formulae can be used if samples are small or if there is no replication.

Matching groups As with the first method it is essential that the groups from whom the regression weights were obtained are relevant.

In-house norms Again, in-house norms are good provided that the numbers are satisfactory.

Problems in the measurement of job success Although it is beyond the scope of a chapter on personality tests, the measurement of job success is in most cases extremely difficult, as Ghiselli (1966) found in a study summarising results from more than 10,000 researches. Thus it has proved extremely difficult to produce a clear criterion of job success for jobs such as school teacher or personnel worker, and this is true of any job where there is no obvious output. However, even where there is, as say with sales persons where volume of sales can be measured, there are difficulties. Thus, in comparing sales of cars through a national network of dealers regional differences, based upon affluence, the location of a dealer relative to other rival dealers and the quality of these rival dealers, should all be taken into account when measuring sales efficiency.

This difficulty of establishing a good criterion of success, especially where success in a job is multidimensional, is a problem in the use of the regression method.

Conclusions

From this it is clear that the regression method can only be used where there are well-sampled occupational groups and where the multiple correlations are high, say 0.7 or greater. However, provided that these conditions are met and further that there is an adequate measure of occupational success, the method is good and has the advantage over the matching method that we know that success rather than simple membership of a group is implicated.

In fact there are few valid personality tests with the requisite regression equations although the 16PF test (Cattell, Eber and Tatsuoko, 1970), despite the problems over the number of factors and despite the fact that some of the equations use samples smaller than desirable, does provide a set of results.

Nevertheless, it must be said about both these methods that as yet there are insufficient test data to make them usable. Ideally as I have argued (Kline, 1992b), an encyclopedia of job specifications would be established where under each job could be found the ideal profile of psychological traits, for the matching method, and a regression equation on to an adequate measure of success, for the regression method. If these data were published, occupational selection could be put onto a statistical and rigorous basis. Since few data of this kind exist, a third method has to be used based upon selecting the right tests.

Selecting the right tests in personnel work From the description of the factor analysis of personality in previous chapters it is clear that four or five variables embrace much of the personality variance – the big five – and in any selection or appraisal procedure it would make good sense to measure these personality factors. This is a sound fall-back procedure. However, this is crude and even the simplest intuitive analysis of jobs suggests that some variables would be more important than others and that the salient variables should be measured. However, this still leaves the question of how we know what the salient variables are.

Task and job analysis In task and job analysis, occupations and jobs are studied in detail to determine as precisely as possible what psychological characteristics are required to carry them out. There are various methods of analysis which I shall describe briefly here and for more details readers should consult Kline (1992b) or Jewell and Siegall (1990). There are three methods.

a Interviews Jewell and Siegall (1990) argue that the best method of finding out what is involved in any job is to ask those who do it. However, the elucidation of reliable information from task analysis interviews is a highly skilled procedure and inexperienced interviewers may emerge with misleading information.

b Observation: task analysis and description In this method a minutely detailed description of exactly what is entailed in carrying out a job is made. When this has been achieved the relevant psychological characteristics are usually obvious. Much of the difficulty in deciding intuitively what is important in a job stems from ignorance of what it entails. This lack of knowledge the task analysis corrects. However, adequate job descriptions require considerable skill and expertise. It is necessary to observe the job being done and to describe it in terms of the purpose of the whole organisation.

Indeed, such detailed task descriptions, based upon observations, should be contrasted with the general job descriptions based on common sense and intuition which are often misleading. For example it is often claimed that accountants need mathematical skills, but job analyses have revealed that the mathematics actually used is not at all difficult. Similarly general job descriptions may fail to reveal crisis points in procedures which detailed analyses ought to identify. One clear example can be seen in the M1 plane crash when an engine caught fire. The cabin crew had no emergency procedures to report this to the flight deck and it was falsely assumed that the pilots could see their engines.

Thus detailed observations of jobs can reveal what psychological traits are required, although it must be remembered that such requirements are only hypotheses which still need confirmatory evidence. Task analyses are still relatively rare, at least in Great Britain, because they are costly and time consuming and relatively few people have been trained to carry them out.

c Questionnaires Because of the problems involved with task analyses and interviews, questionnaires are often used to assess the demands of different jobs. One of the best of these is the Position Analysis Questionnaire, the PAQ (McCormick *et al.*, 1972), which I shall briefly describe.

The PAQ has 194 items relating to five aspects of a job: work output, mental processes, information input, relationships with other people, and a general category of other characteristics. Factor analytic studies suggest that twelve dimensions are measured by the PAQ, including variables such as decision making, operating a machine, performing routine activities – all dimensions, as Jewell and Siegall (1990) point out, which are somewhat common-sense. It is a useful measure although some jobs seem not to fit its categories and a further version has been produced for professional occupations.

Conclusions Task analysis and description is the best method of ascertaining the demands of jobs. However, this is costly and requires skilled personnel. In their absence the PAQ is better than nothing as a basis to select tests. Ideally, tests should be selected on empirical grounds, that is that they have been shown to correlate with success at the job or reliably discriminate members of an occupational group. However, there is one further point that should not be forgotten.

Use of criterion-keyed tests

As has been stressed in the discussion of personality tests throughout this book, factored variables have psychological meaning once the factors have been identified, whereas criterion-keyed tests, which may discriminate occupational groups, have no necessary psychological meaning and are usually mixtures of disparate variables. This means that if factored tests are used in the applied field, all results have psychological meaning and psychological knowledge can gradually be increased as more and more results are collected. However, if criterion-keyed tests are used, there is no accretion of knowledge and as jobs change and new jobs come into being the tests become useless. Thus where possible, except for mass screening, the use of criterion-keyed tests should be avoided.

Other issues in the use of personality tests in personnel work

Kline (1992a, 1992b) has a detailed examination of a variety of issues involved in the use of tests in personnel work of which the most important will be discussed here.

Faking and deliberate distortion This is obviously a problem in all work situations, even in appraisal, but especially selection, when subjects know that their careers are at stake. Personality questionnaires are not difficult to fake. Thus few serious applicants for a sales position would admit to being shy or nervous with people. This is why Cattell and Warburton (1967) advocate the use of objective tests which are resistant to faking, although, as has been seen, they are not well enough validated to be used in applied work.

Most tests have lie scales for detecting those who are distorting or faking scores. However, all that can be done if such individuals are detected in a selection process is to ignore their scores on the grounds that they are likely to be inaccurate. It is not possible to correct scores for distortions.

Ipsative scores Ipsative scores, based upon forced choices, should not be used in selection procedures. Scores of different subjects are not comparable and thus comparisons are senseless. For this reason norms are not meaningful even if they are supplied with ipsative tests. Ipsative scores are suited only to discussion with individual subjects and this will be dealt with in a later section on the use of personality tests in appraisal.

Ethics and confidentiality of scores Under the Data Protection Act if the scores of subjects are stored on computer they have the right to see them. If they are not the question arises as to whether subjects should have access to their scores. This is not an objective matter but one of personal judgement.

In my view there is no reason to withhold scores from a subject. It infringes no personal freedom of a subject to know her scores and it is difficult to produce any argument to sustain withholding scores. A counter-argument which is sometimes offered by practitioners is that subjects might misunderstand the results, and thus feedback might produce problems.

Computer reports from tests This argument will not do. If psychologists believe that scores may be misunderstood then they must explicate them. This is a lengthy process but given the easy availability of computer reports where large numbers of candidates are involved, these should be used. It is possible to administer questionnaires on microcomputer. The items are presented on the computer screen and the responses are made on the keyboard. This has the advantage that scoring can be automatic and immediate and a print-out of the results with an interpretation can be also immediately available. These results are based on an expert system in which the data in the test manual are stored in the computer thus enabling comparison with norms to be made. There are difficulties in ensuring that the computer reports are satisfactory, especially where scores have bad connotations, but these can be overcome with care.

It should be noted that computer-administered tests should be shown to produce similar results to the original pencil and paper form. It should also be realised that the results of tests administered in the standard way can be fed into a computer and similar print-outs based on the test manuals can be provided.

In brief, feedback should always be given to candidates after the selection process and the use of computer reports makes this possible even with large numbers of candidates.

As a final point, it is important, also, that candidates feel confident that the results of testing will remain confidential to those engaged in the selection process.

Use of personality tests in appraisal

I shall deal briefly with this topic because almost everything which has been written so far about the use of personality tests in personnel work applies equally to selection and appraisal. Thus in appraisal (where test results form the basis of a discussion about individuals' career prospects) it is essential that the tests are as valid and as relevant to the posts and as reliable as they are in selection. The better the test the better the appraisal. However, there are some differences, mainly of emphasis, in using tests in appraisal rather than selection and these will be discussed below.

Validity of tests Although, as has been argued, tests should be valid, in appraisal less valid tests can be used, provided that lack of validity is borne in mind. Thus tests can be used as useful bases for discussion rather than for the precision of their scores. This is certainly true of interest and motivational tests.

Ipsative scores Although ipsative scores are not useful for selection they are valuable in appraisal. Thus the fact that a subject has ranked one score higher than another is a legitimate basis of discussion. Appraisal is the main arena for ipsatively scored tests.

Feedback As is obvious, appraisal is all about feedback. Essentially the scores, where they are trustworthy, and the test items where the tests are less efficient, are the bases of discussion rather than firm decision making. Thus for example, if a subject is highly extraverted this can be discussed with her and the possibility of working in a position where extravert qualities are important can be examined.

Conclusions concerning personality tests in personnel work From this discussion it is clear that personality tests are valuable in personnel selection and appraisal. Ideally, factored tests should be given to good samples of different occupational groups so that the regression and matching methods can be used. In addition, task analyses and descriptions of jobs should be undertaken so that the requisite personality tests can be selected. Finally the importance of feedback, especially in appraisal, was stressed.

The use of personality tests in clinical and educational psychology

Clinical psychology

I shall deal first with clinical psychology, although, as shall become clear, there is a considerable overlap with educational psychology, which is why they appear in the same section of this chapter.

Definition of clinical psychology Clinical psychology refers to that branch of psychology which is concerned with the treatment and understanding of mental disorders. In fact this can be broken down into diagnosis, assessment of treatment and clinical theory and personality tests have a part to play in all of these aspects of the field.

Use of different types of personality tests

Personality inventories As was noted above with reference to occupational psychology, the distinction between factored tests and criterion-keyed tests is particularly important in clinical psychology and for much the same reasons as were discussed previously. The great advantage of factor analytic personality inventories is that the variables are psychologically meaningful with the result that all findings can be used in the development of clinical theory. In contrast, the results from criterion-keyed scales are difficult if not impossible to interpret and psychological generalisation is correspondingly problematic. This is particularly ironic since the most commonly used personality test in clinical psychology is the MMPI (Hathaway and McKinley, 1951) and its updated version MMPI–2 (Graham, 1990), both criterion-keyed tests.

Projective tests In Chapter 2 the problems with projective tests, their lack of reliability and validity, were discussed and it had to be concluded that they were not satisfactory for the scientific analysis of personality although objective scoring schemes might be able to remedy some of the deficiencies. As a result of these psychometric defects, the results from the clinical application of projective tests do not enter into the psychometric view of personality despite the fact that the Rorschach test has been extensively used in this field. However, because projective personality tests play so large a part in clinical psychology some mention of the results will be found in a brief section of this chapter.

Objective tests These tests which, as was made clear in Chapter 2, are still largely of unknown validity, are potentially powerful in clinical psychology since, in principle at least, they are measuring meaningful factors. However, in practice, with insufficient evidence of validity, interpretation of clinical results is difficult.

On these grounds much of this section on the contribution of the psychometric view of personality to clinical psychology will be concerned with the relevant findings from personality inventories, especially those measuring clear factors.

Clinical diagnosis

Although diagnosis in clinical psychology is regarded by some psychologists as anathema, being an example of an outmoded medical model and of labelling clients to their disadvantage, in fact diagnosis is essential for the scientific study of psychological disorders. Only by accurate diagnosis can psychologists feel confident that they are talking about the same condition, when they are investigating causal factors and the efficacy of treatments.

Factored personality tests in clinical psychology As has been discussed throughout this book, factor analysis has identified the most important factors in the personality sphere. The big five factors, extraversion, anxiety, tough-mindedness, conscientiousness and open-mindedness, can usually be found in questionnaires among normal subjects and Cattell (e.g. 1973) isolated a number of abnormal factors which are not so well replicated. However, because the emergence of the big five factors is relatively recent, there is little fundamental clinical work with these factors. Indeed two psychologists stand out in their attempts to utilise the findings from the factor analysis of personality tests in clinical psychology – Eysenck and Cattell – and consequently much of the work discussed below concerns their factors.

The work of Cattell

In principle, as Cattell and colleagues have argued (Bolton, 1986), there are two approaches to clinical diagnosis using factored tests. These have been discussed in the previous section on the use of tests in selection and will be briefly mentioned here.

The regression method Here the multiple regression is computed between the diagnostic group and the personality test scores. The weights from the regression equation are used in the computation of the client's score. The highest score represents the diagnostic category.

The matching method Here the profile of scores on the personality test of various clinical groups is matched to the profile of scores of the client. The best match represents the diagnosis. Cattell has developed a special pattern similarity coefficient to ease the computation.

As was also mentioned in the previous chapter, the efficacy of both these methods depends on adequate sampling of the diagnostic groups. In addition, in the regression method it is essential that a satisfactory multiple correlation was obtained and that the beta weights were replicated. In the matching method it is important that there are clear differences between the profiles of the groups. If all these conditions are fulfilled then these methods are powerful. What they both reveal are the personality factors which discriminate the diagnostic clinical groups.

Advantages of these methods The great advantage of using these methods with factored personality tests is that because the psychological meaning of these factors and their importance in personality is established, all results are themselves meaningful. Thus if it turns out that extraversion discriminates a particular clinical group then this is important in understanding the nature of the disorder, and similarly with other factors.

In fact Cattell and his colleagues have collected together a considerable body of findings with the 16PF normal factors and the abnormal factors of the CAQ (Krug, 1980), as well as with the MAT (Cattell, Horn and Sweney, 1970), a motivation test and the objective OAB (Cattell and Schuerger, 1976).

As has been pointed out in previous chapters of this book, the validity of the Cattell personality tests, both of temperament and motivation, has been called into question so that the substantive findings from this work must remain questionable. Thus the main contribution of Cattell to this field must be one of principle and method. There can be no doubt that his approach of using factored variables to discriminate diagnostic and clinical groups is potentially powerful once the major factors of personality have been identified. On account of his brilliant and pioneering efforts in the clinical field his main findings deserve a brief summary. For greater detail readers must be referred to Bolton (1986).

According to Bolton (1986) it can be argued from the work with the 16PF test that diagnosed neurosis (incidentally a very broad category) is caused by a combination of six primary source traits: low ego strength (C), submissiveness (low E), desurgency (low F), emotional sensitivity (I), guilt (O) and excessive ergic tension (Q4). It should not escape readers that this factor analytic diagnosis of neurosis resembles to a remarkable degree the basic psychoanalytic claims that neurosis results from the repression of a too powerful superego. The high Q4 and O and the low C fit peculiarly well. This agreement between the entirely speculative approach of psychoanalysis and the rigorous statistics of factor analysis is indeed striking. In addition using the second-order factors it can be shown that neurotics are, compared with normals, high on the anxiety factor and low on extraversion.

Another important finding from the application of factor analytic personality tests in the abnormal field supports the claim that in most instances, psychopathology can be seen as an extreme of a normal continuum. Neurotics in general have personalities that are not qualitatively different from those of normals.

This is particularly interesting because in the case of the psychoses (abnormal syndromes characterised by lack of contact with reality and best exemplified by the schizophrenias) this is not the case. Here the discriminating factors are not found in normal personality and are those factors measured by the CAQ (Krug, 1980) which was described in Chapter 5. Thus psychotics are qualitatively different from normals. For example, schizophrenics are characterised by high scores on depressed withdrawal and on the schizophrenic scale itself which deals with extreme withdrawal from reality.

Again it is interesting to note that this distinction between neurotics and psychotics fits well with psychoanalytic theory in which neurosis is seen as the result of ego defences which all normals use while psychosis occurs when the ego defences are overwhelmed.

At this point, mention should be made of depth psychometry which has been well described by Heather Cattell (1986). The principle of depth psychometry claims that the same general neurotic symptoms may result from different configurations of the primary source traits which are implicated in neurosis. This configuration is important because, as has been argued, source traits, as revealed by factor analysis, are the underlying determinants of the observed variations in human personality. These, in the case of abnormal psychology, are the descriptive syndromes such as anxiety neurosis or depression. Thus depth psychometry, by analysing the underlying source traits, enables the psychologist to understand rather than simply describe the diagnostic categories.

Furthermore, the fact that normal factors are implicated in neurotic syndromes and abnormal factors in psychotic disorders immediately suggests the importance of these factors for the assessment of therapeutic progress. Thus in the case of neurotics, as treatment proceeds the elevated scores on the normal factors should gradually approach the normal band. Similarly in the case of psychotics, scores on the abnormal factors should approach zero, since these factors are rarely seen in normals.

Bolton (1986) reports similarly powerful discriminations of neurotic disorders with the T factors from an objective personality test – the Objective Analytic Battery, the OAB (Cattell and Schuerger, 1976). However, I shall not discuss these findings here because the validity of this test is not well supported partly because it has not been widely used. Indeed, a study of the validity of this test by Kline and Cooper (1984b) was not at all encouraging, as was discussed in Chapter 4. However, in principle, if valid objective personality tests could be devised they would be valuable in abnormal psychology, used as has been described above.

Cattell's motivational factors, as measured by the MAT (Cattell, Horn and Sweney, 1970), a test described in Chapter 6, have also been employed in the study of abnormal groups. The MAT factors can be placed into regression equations or matched to the profiles of clinical groups, just as was the case with the temperamental factors. Indeed, all these tests form part of the psychometric model together with ability factors. However, as Bolton (1986) has argued, the motivational factors have been used in a different way. Again my description will be brief since there are difficulties with the validity of the MAT, as was shown by Cooper and Kline (1982).

The underlying dynamics of patients in the different diagnostic categories can be worked out. For this, P factors are computed for each individual (involving the factoring of scores over occasions) and these are then inserted into the dynamic calculus which indicates how drives are expressed in behaviour, a quantified psychoanalysis according to Cattell (1985). Although the mathematics of this dynamic calculus are exceedingly complex, a simple illustration will clarify its essence. If P analysis revealed that in a particular individual the sex erg loaded on a factor which included activities such as carrying out factor analyses and writing short stories it would imply that these activities had sexual roots, as indeed, psychoanalysis supposes. In this way the dynamics of behaviour can be revealed.

Since the dynamic calculus is highly abstruse and since it is not accepted other than by Cattell and his colleagues and since there is doubt, as has been argued, concerning the validity of these ergs and sentiments, no more details of these methods will be given. Nevertheless despite these problems, the principles of the dynamic calculus are brilliant and original and if better measures could be developed this approach would be extremely powerful.

There is one final use of factored tests in clinical psychology which deserves brief mention. This concerns their application in the study of therapeutic success. One example has already been mentioned, namely that as treatment proceeds, we should expect the elevated scores on the salient factors to return to the normal level. This is useful and important. However, there is a far more sophisticated approach to the problem of therapeutic recovery.

This involves putting into factor analyses measures of temperament and dynamics together with details of what went on in the therapy, type of therapist, current events in the life of the patient and therapeutic outcome. From the variables loading on therapeutic outcome it would be possible to answer questions which dog clinical psychology, such as the effect of life events, type of therapist and therapeutic interventions. Unfortunately, owing to the dislike of quantification among the majority of clinical psychologists, no such studies have as yet been carried out, although case work with the Cattell factors (Heather Cattell, 1986) strongly supports this approach. Since it is possible that some of the links in these processes are not linear but involve interactions, more complex analyses such as are found in structural modelling (Joreskog and Sorbom, 1979) might be valuable.

Conclusions This discussion of the use by Cattell and colleagues of

Cattell's factored tests indicates clearly the brilliance of Cattell's work both in relation to diagnosis and to treatment. These methods could lead, as was suggested, to a quantified psychoanalysis. However, the fact that the tests are probably not valid, except for the second-order personality inventory factors, means that substantive findings are to be treated with caution. However, it should be said that as better tests are developed they could be used with the methods which have been discussed in the development of an effective psychometric clinical psychology.

The work of Eysenck

Eysenck and his colleagues at the Maudsley have carried out considerable clinical research with their factors, E, N and P, as measured by the EPQ. These of course, as has been argued, have extensive evidence for validity, are second-order factors and are three of the big five factors which regularly occur in personality questionnaires. It should also be noted that the first two of these factors are identical with the first two second-order Cattell factors – exvia and anxiety.

In respect of E and N the findings are highly similar to those of Cattell with these second-order factors. Neurotics tend to be unstable introverts. Of course in the Eysenck system N is regarded as arising from lability of the autonomic nervous system (Eysenck, 1967), while extraversion is conceived as stemming from the arousability of the central nervous system, and it is alleged by Eysenck (1976) that extraverts are more difficult to condition than introverts, and that the differences between abnormal groups on these two factors are accounted for by these physiological factors.

The P, psychoticism, or tough-mindedness factor is particularly interesting. As Eysenck and Eysenck (1976) demonstrated, P discriminates as surely as does N, psychiatric groups from normals. Psychotic patients (made up mostly of schizophrenics) and prisoners have the highest scores, followed by drug addicts, patients with personality disorders and sex offenders. Furthermore, although the P scale is not a symptom list, severity of symptoms is positively correlated with P.

In discussing these findings the power of using meaningful factored scales, rather than criterion-keyed tests of unknown psychological meaning, becomes apparent. Thus, for example, the N factor is also good at discriminating clinical groups, in this case mainly neurotic groups. However, P and N are orthogonal, uncorrelated. From this discussion the following conclusions may be drawn.

Neuroses and psychoses are not on the same continuum. Thus neurotics score more highly than normals on N, psychotics on P. This means that psychotic and neurotic disorders are qualitatively different. Psychosis is not simply an exaggerated neurosis. Actually Claridge (1985) has developed an excellent psychometric measure of schizotypic personality with which he has shown that there are certain schizophrenic-like symptoms possessed by normals which are exaggerated in both schizophenics and gifted, creative individuals. On this psychometric basis he has developed an impressive theoretical account of the development of schizophrenia. His work is an excellent example of the value of psychometrics in clinical psychology even though it is likely that the schizotypal personality is not factorially clear.

Since, as was discussed in Chapter 7, all these factors have a considerable genetic determination, all these results are of considerable theoretical interest for clinical psychology. It certainly appears that these three personality factors are highly important in the development of neurotic and psychotic disorders and hence in their treatment. Any adequate clinical theories must take them into account. It must be concluded even from this brief discussion of the contribution of Eysenck to clinical diagnosis that the psychometric view of personality is of great psychological significance.

Findings from other personality tests

In a book in which clinical psychology is only a small section it would not be possible to discuss all the results of the administration of personality tests in the clinical field. However, as has been made clear, the main contribution comes from factored tests which by definition deal with the most important variables in the field. Nevertheless certain non-factored personality tests have been so widely used in clinical psychology that their results must be examined.

The MMPI and MMPI–2

These tests were described in Chapter 6 and in Chapter 2 where it was pointed out that despite the fact that the original test, the MMPI, was the most widely used personality inventory, the fact that it was criterion-keyed rendered the scales empty of psychological meaning. Thus the mass of clinical findings reported with this test have made and can make little contribution to knowledge of clinical psychology. All that can be said is that an MMPI scale (and more than 200 have been developed from the original item pool, Dahlstrom and Walsh, 1960) can or cannot discriminate particular criterion groups. Unfortunately the same is true of the newly developed MMPI–2 (Graham, 1990).

Proponents of the MMPI can argue that for some purposes discrimination is all that is required. Thus if perhaps in army selection it is necessary to screen out all neurotics or psychotics, an efficient criterion-keyed test such as the MMPI is highly useful. While this is true, it should be pointed out that there is no reason why a battery of factored tests should not be equally efficient at screening out clinical cases and in this case some understanding of the psychological nature of the problems would have been gained.

Since, in addition, the diagnosis of clinical groups is a problem in itself and is highly unreliable (Beck, 1962) the whole basis of the original keying of the MMPI items is a difficulty. This together with the fact that the scales are not reliable and have overlapping items also renders the psychometric qualities of the MMPI dubious.

Since the test is so widely used in clinical psychology, attempts have been made to factor it and thus render it a more useful test, as was discussed in Chapter 5. At the scale level there is general agreement that two factors account for much of the variance – anxiety and ego strength (Friedman *et al.*, 1989) – factors which come as no surprise given the fact that these are implicated in the clinical work with the 16PF test, discussed above.

Rather than scales, parcels of items were factored by Cattell and colleagues and some of these factors were used in the CAQ (Krug, 1980) which attempts to measure the main abnormal factors and which has been described in this chapter. Probably the ability of the MMPI to discriminate clinical groups depends on these factors.

Johnson *et al.* (1984) factored the MMPI items using 11,000 subjects. They obtained a large number of factors which generally grouped together the items with similar meanings. However, they were identified simply from their item content with no external validity and thus this identification must remain uncertain. However, they identified anxiety, psychoticism and extraversion, all part of the big five and paranoia, psychopathic deviation and psychasthenia which are included in the CAQ (Krug, 1980). Costa *et al.* (1985) also claim to have found the big five, as they do in every test, in the MMPI items. Finally it should be noted that Graham (1990) argues that the Johnson *et al.* (1984) factors are probably to be found in the MMPI–2.

Conclusions Despite the wide use of the MMPI in clinical studies and the updating of the MMPI–2 it is difficult to justify the work. It is only suitable for screening and the lack of meaning of the scales makes it inferior to factored tests. The clinical contribution of psychometrics cannot arise from either of these tests or from any criterion-keyed tests. That it measures factors is fortuitous and results from the skilful choice of items in the original item pool. However, these factors are better measured by tests deliberately designed to do so. The best of the MMPI is to be found in the second part of the CAQ. In brief, a test that has not contributed to the psychometric view of personality in abnormal psychology.

The Rorschach Test

This projective test (Rorschach, 1921) is one of the most famous personality tests known beyond the confines of psychology. Rorschach developed this series of ten inkblots specifically for clinical work and over the years there have been thousands of clinical studies and some different versions of the test have been constructed.

However, as was discussed in Chapter 2 the Rorschach is not reliable and has poor evidence for validity. However, G analysis of Rorschach data (Holley, 1973) where objectively scored Rorschach protocols are subjected to multivariate analysis might prove useful in the clinical context. So far little of substantive value has been attained by these methods but they are worthy of further research because they make use of the rich data which are yielded by projective tests. Furthermore these projective data, as has been argued in Chapter 2, may be valuable since some researchers appear to be able to use them effectively. It should also be pointed out that Exner (1986) has attempted to put Rorschach scoring on a more objective footing, while keeping within the boundaries of normal projective test scoring. Even so there is not strong evidence for the validity of Rorschach interpretations.

In brief, at present it cannot be argued that the Rorschach has made a powerful contribution to the psychology of personality either normal or abnormal and it is unlikely to do so until reliable quantification is introduced.

Conclusions From this discussion of two of the most famous non-factored tests commonly used in clinical psychology, it is clear that little psychological knowledge has come from them. The advantages of using factored tests with externally validated psychologically meaningful factors become obvious when the problems of the MMPI and Rorschach are discussed.

Contributions to clinical theory

There are two contributions to clinical psychology from psychometrics. The first and less important is as a test of other clinical theories. Thus if, as is the case with ergs and sentiments discovered by factor analysis (Cattell, 1985), it appears that there are ten important motivational factors, then clinical theories which deal with motivation and which posit a different number of variables are shown to be incorrect. To continue with this example Freudian theory has two drives, sex and aggression, or later Eros and Thanatos. These are underestimates. McDougall (1932) and Murray (1938) considerably overestimate the numbers of drives. Again, writers such as McClelland (1961) who stress the importance of need achievement have probably made too much of this variable.

A second and potentially more valuable use of the psychometric factor analytic findings in personality is to construct clinical theories on the basis of the actual results. The rationale for this is that the simple structure factors are, as has been argued, the salient variables in the field. This being the case any adequate theory must account for them. In clinical psychology it has been shown, must for example, that Eysenck's extraversion, neuroticism and psychoticism are salient variables in the discrimination of neurotics and psychotics and any theory of abnormal psychology must, therefore, include these factors as critical variables.

Indeed, the specification equations of personality factors for clinical diagnostic groups, if the multiple correlations are high, effectively constitute theories. Thus if three personality factors can predict that an individual is a depressive, then these are all that is necessary to understand the condition.

So far in clinical psychology, owing to the problems of isolating the best set of personality factors, substantive findings from the specification equations have not yet been made, although the attempts to do this by Cattell are models of how a genuine clinical psychometric theory could be constructed. Actually, in the next chapter, we shall see how Eysenck and Cattell have attempted to develop more general psychometric theories of personality based upon their factor analytic results.

Educational psychology

Educational psychology is concerned with the psychological problems affecting educational progress and achievement. Thus to some extent there is bound to be some overlap with clinical psychology, if emotional difficulties are at the root of educational problems, and with occupational psychology when questions of selection and vocational guidance arise.

In this section of this chapter I shall briefly set out what personality tests have to offer to various problems central to educational psychology as it has been defined above.

The failing child Educational psychologists are frequently asked to investigate the causes of failure in children, when their teachers are at a loss to account for the poor performance. I do not want here to make exaggerated claims as to the importance of personality tests in this aspect of educational psychology. As is fully documented in any modern text of educational psychology (e.g. Fontana, 1981) there are various factors which can affect a child's performance at school: attitude of parents to school; attitude of peers to school; having somewhere quiet to work; emotional problems of the child; level of intellectual ability; quality of the school, just for example.

Given these complex and doubtless interacting factors at work in determining academic performance, it may well be doubted whether there is any useful role for personality testing. In fact there is a small but limited place for personality testing, although this is restricted to factored personality tests because only these have the necessary reliability and validity. Projective and objective tests are not satisfactory except as research instruments in this field.

The rationale for the value of personality tests in this aspect of educational psychology is to be found in the extensive work that was carried out in the 1960s and 1970s in predicting academic success, much of which is summarised in Kline (1979; Cattell and Kline, 1977). In almost all cases the tests used were those of Cattell and Eysenck, which, as has been discussed, are among the best factored measures. Here it was found that at the primary school, mildly neurotic extraverts did best, while at the secondary level the anxious introvert was successful. At university the findings are essentially similar to secondary school, not only in the West but in cultures such as India and Africa, for example Ghana (Kline, 1966). Particularly important in these studies is the work of Cattell and Butcher (1968) who put into a multiple regression with academic success at the secondary school, tests of ability, personality and motivation, thus allowing the relative predictive power of these variables to be assessed. The critical points to note about these results are that the correlations with personality and motivational factors, while significant, are small, in the region of 0.2 to 0.3, and that the contribution of the three types of factor – ability, temperamental and dynamic – is separate and distinct. Thus Cattell and Butcher (1968) found a multiple correlation of 0.6 with academic success which is about as high as it could be if there are any effects at all of school and environment on academic performance.

Given the small size of the individual correlations between success and dynamic and temperamental factors, interpretations of the scores of any individual would have to be extremely cautious. Furthermore the personality tests would have to be interpreted in the light of the results of ability tests. Thus if a child was simply not bright enough for a highly academic school, this is sufficient reason for difficulties. If, however, failure is not attributable to this or any other important family or domestic factors, as far as can be ascertained, then it makes sense to examine the personality and motivational factors which are correlated to academic success. For example, if it turns out that a child is highly extravert, that might at least in part be a contributory cause of difficulty. Here, it might be helpful to put the child in as extraverted an atmosphere as was possible at the school, for example with the most lively and noisy teachers.

Sometimes personality testing can reveal that a child is highly anxious. Although it is difficult to remedy this, teachers can bear this in mind in the way they treat the child and this might produce some improvement. As a final example, it could be that a child has a low N score. Now this, as has been seen in the correlation with anxiety, is not conducive to high academic performance, presumably because if students are low on anxiety they do not worry if assignments are not completed nor are they galvanised into study by the imminence of examinations. These small correlations with anxiety do not suggest, incidentally, that high anxiety is good for academic success. It is almost certainly not. Rather there is a moderate facilitating level which tends to make students work hard, worry about failure and seek to remedy their failings – all leading to enhanced examination performance.

From this discussion it is clear that there is a part to play for factored personality tests in the diagnosis and treatment of educational difficulties although all test scores must be interpreted in the light of the abilities of the students and their other personal circumstances.

Educational selection The fact that there are significant correlations between academic success and Cattell's temperamental and dynamic factors (which do not overlap with ability factors) indicates clearly that in any rational selection system for education these personality factors would have to be included.

In the handbook to the 16PF test, regression equations for academic success at university can be found and these would be used exactly as was suggested for the regression equations in occupational selection. However, it is clear that more work is required in this field since the four regressions in the text have somewhat different weights, although the multiple correlations are substantial. These fluctuations are probably related to the unreliability of the Cattell factors, as has been discussed.

The fact that the individual correlations with the primary factors are small and that the weights vary from study to study means that in practice it is better to include the second-order factors or the big five factors which have been shown to embrace much of the reliable personality variance. If this were done it would probably eliminate those whose personality was unsuited to academic pursuits – extreme extraverts, the highly anxious and the high P scorers. Those who were high on conscientiousness would be favoured by such a system and this is correct since, in our present educational system, these individuals do well relative to their abilities.

In an egalitarian age such as ours, the notion of including personality tests for selection to education is undoubtedly impractical, since there is resistance even to the application of IQ tests when there can be no doubt that educability depends to a considerable extent on intelligence (Jensen, 1980). Nevertheless, given the correlations, if personality tests were used in selection procedures together, of course, with tests of ability, overall selection would be more efficient.

Vocational guidance I shall not say much here about the use of personality tests in vocational guidance because the basis of so doing is identical with that in occupational selection which has been discussed in detail at the beginning of the chapter. Exactly as was there argued, the psychometric model underpinning the use of all psychological tests suggests that there is an ideal configuration of personality traits for each job. These, therefore, have to be discovered and then each individual can be tested to find the job that is most appropriate.

Thus personality testing is an essential part of vocational guidance. It is not the place in this chapter to discuss in detail how the personality test scores should be used for vocational guidance (see Kline, 1975, 1992a). Suffice it to say that they would form the basis for discussion with the children rather than being used in a rigid statistical formulation, as sometimes occurs in selection. However, there is no doubt that those factored personality and motivation tests which correlate highly with occupational success or discriminate clearly different occupational groups are critical variables to be discussed in any efficient system of vocational guidance.

Educational theory

I shall now discuss the contribution from the psychometric analysis of personality to educational theory. Gillis (1986) attempts this task in relation to the Cattell personality factors but his arguments are applicable in principle to other factors. He takes the regression equations of the 16PF tests for academic success (discussed in the section on selection) and those of the HSPQ (the high-school version of the 16PF) where it appears that superego and self-sentiment are the best predictors. These are, of course, dynamic variables as well and when measured as such in the MAT they also have the highest weights.

Clearly, as Gillis (1986) argues, these findings should be incorporated into any theory which attempts to account for educational success. In fact, it fits the work of McDougall (1932) who regarded superego and self-sentiment as master sentiments, the keys to understanding human dynamics. While this is so, it must be pointed out that such findings cannot be used to prove this theory since proof requires refutation not confirmation (Popper, 1959). Of course, factored results can be used to refute any theory or to provide support, as this example illustrates.

In addition they can be used to develop a psychometric theory. Indeed, both Eysenck (1967) and Cattell (1981) have attempted to fit their findings into a theoretical framework. However, this is broad and general rather than specific to educational psychology and as such it will be discussed in the next chapter.

Conclusions

In this section the salience of personality testing in educational psychology has been made clear. Meaningful, factored personality tests have a small part to play in the study of individual problems in educational success and can undoubtedly improve the efficiency of educational selection. They are essential for vocational guidance and can be useful in the development of educational theory.

Chapter 9

Personality theory and the psychometrics of personality

As has been argued throughout this book, the psychometric view of personality is based upon the results of psychometric personality tests, not all tests however, but factor analytic tests, where the factors have been externally validated and are not simply collections of semantically similar items. Such factors are, from the nature of factor analysis itself, the most important variables in the field because they account for the maximum variance. Thus if factor analysis has been properly executed – adequate sampling of tests and variables, the selection of the correct number of factors, rotation to simple structure (and possibly further confirmatory analysis) followed by external identification of the factors – it must be the case that resulting factors are the salient variables and, therefore, the ones that must be central in any theory of personality.

With this view of factors it is clear that the factor analysis of personality bears upon personality theory in two ways. On the one hand it is highly pertinent to all theories of personality, of which, as was pointed out in the introductory chapter, there is a very large number. Any theory which does not deal with the main factors must be missing the point. On the other hand, a psychometric personality theory can be developed utilising the main factors from the analyses.

In this chapter on personality theory both these aspects of the work will be considered, and I shall deal first with the bearing of the results on personality theories. It is not possible or even desirable to examine the bearing of the factor analyses of personality on all personality theories, since many theories of personality, especially those developed early in this century, are little more than interesting speculations (and often they are not even interesting). However, I shall consider the most famous and influential of these theories, which are not obviously shown to be false by other current developments in psychology, together with some of the more recent accounts which are popular in modern texts on personality (e.g. Pervin, 1990).

The scientific status of factors

Before the bearing of the findings from the factor analysis of personality on personality theories can be evaluated it is necessary to scrutinise the status of factors a little more carefully. So far in this book the strictly statistical view has been argued that factors are a set of dimensions which account for the intercorrelations among the original variables. As Cattell (1978) has argued in cases where the factors are known, from theories of physics for example, simple structure factor analyses are able to find these factors, and they can be regarded as causal determinants. Nevertheless, the status of personality factors in a field where the notion of determiners is not so clear cut, requires further examination.

To clarify the points I shall deal with one factor, extraversion, rather than the whole set, although, of course, the arguments apply equally to all personality factors.

Extraversion can be thought of as a construct which accounts for a good proportion of variance in personality questionnaires. More specifically, it accounts for the intercorrelations between certain kinds of items: those concerned with enjoying parties, being sociable, liking people and excitement and so on. In this sense extraversion might be said to have a causal function.

However, what does it mean to say that extraversion is a personality factor? It is clear that extraversion is not a physical object such as a brain or an eye. At no point will neuroscientists be able to open the skull and point to extraversion. Extraversion is a concept, or construct, defined not verbally but by its factor loadings. It is a concept, therefore, of higher precision than one simply verbally defined. In science, constructs are no less important than physical objects which, of course, are also constructs. With no concept of brain for example, it could not be separated from the head or regarded as a single entity and not a collection of neurons. An example of a highly useful concept in biology is that of Man. This includes all groups of *Homo sapiens*, regardless of skin colour or height for example, variables in which there are considerable variations, and other now extinct forms. Now there is no object Man which could ever be observed, although the concept is essential in understanding the development of many human characteristics. It should be pointed out at this point that if a large number of biological characteristics of mammals were subjected to factor analysis, the major Linnaean groups; primates, carnivores, and –

within them, dogs and cats for example – would undoubtedly emerge as factors. Just as these factors account for mammalian physical characteristics, so extraversion is essential in understanding the fact that certain traits are found together, as well as other important aspects of personality as will be discussed later in this section, especially when the work of Eysenck is described. In other words, the fact that extraversion is a concept does not mean that it is scientifically valueless. This is particularly so since personality itself is an abstract concept. Indeed most of psychology, especially the study of personality, is a field of abstract concepts rather than physical objects. The physical in psychology is the province of anatomy and neurology and it is arguable that this primarily conceptual nature of the subject makes it unsuitable to the methods of the natural sciences. This indeed was the view of the behaviourists who attempted to remedy the fault by studying only observable behaviour. Nevertheless, since science does deal with abstractions, this is probably too pessimistic a view.

There are several advantages of factor analytically defined concepts compared with verbal notions. One mentioned above is precision. Factor loadings are numerical and the tests are specified. Verbal definitions are notoriously slippery. The second and more significant advantage, is rooted in the nature of factor analysis. Factors are important because they account for variance. Now it is possible to develop concepts by speculation or philosophy which empirically turn out to be trivial or misleading. To take again some obvious biological examples, it would be possible to classify mammals (if that was a recognisable category) by fur colour of by density of fur. The length and presence of tails might be another classificatory factor. These, as it turns out, are entirely superficial and trivial characteristics in understanding different mammalian forms. Now it could well be the case, since the psychology of personality is still in an elementary state, for there is little agreement in the field, that many of the variables and concepts in use are similarly superficial and trivial.

The main personality factors

As was made clear in Chapter 4, five personality factors appear to account for the variance in most personality questionnaires. Of these the three most important, and the backbone of Eysenck's system, have the highest validity of any personality measures and their external correlates are particularly well supported. These factors are: extraversion, neuroticism and psychoticism or tough-mindedness, factors at the second-order to be found in the system of Cattell. The other two of the big five factors are open-mindedness and conscientiousness. Clearly, as has been argued, any viable personality theory must incorporate these factors as important variables.

As was made clear, the dynamic factors revealed by factor analysis are not so well supported as the temperamental factors. Only Cattell (1985) has carried out systematic factor analytic research into personality dynamics. Despite the relative uncertainty of the list of ergs and sentiments, these results are still useful in assessing the worth of dynamic theories of personality, although their results have to be treated with more caution than is the case with the temperamental factors. Cattell's work on the strength of interest factors should also not be forgotten although this is even more problematic than the work on the structure of drives.

Freudian theory Whatever the virtues of Freudian personality theory, as found in Freud (1933), among them cannot be found the explication of these factors. For psychoanalysis, overt personality is to be seen as resulting from the efforts of the ego, especially defence mechanisms, to hold the dynamic equilibrium between ego, superego and id. In this conception of personality there is no place for these three factors.

Of course, Freudian psychoanalysis is a complex theory. Another aspect of Freudian personality theory is developmental. Thus fixation at certain levels of development, psychosexual phases (Freud, 1905), was said to lead to the development of oral, anal or phallic characters.

Kline (1981) has studied in detail the psychometric evidence concerning these Freudian personality syndromes and has developed and validated measures of the anal and oral character (Kline, 1971; Kline and Storey, 1977). If the putative psychosexual origins of these personality constellations (hence their names) are ignored, there still remains the question as to whether such syndromes can be observed. It could be the case that Freud had correctly observed the personality characteristics but quite wrongly inferred their developmental bases.

In fact it appears that there are two personality syndromes, oral pessimism and oral optimism, that correspond well to the oral character and one that fits closely the anal character, although there is little evidence to relate these syndromes to infantile experience, other than a study by Kline (1968) in which the scores on Ai3Q, a measure of anal traits, correlated positively to a quite different measure of anality – that of the Blacky Pictures (Blum, 1949) which portrays a defecating dog. This was an interesting finding rather than compelling evidence for the link. Factor analytic studies of these syndromes showed that, despite the outlandish names, there was no little resemblance to the main psychometric factors described in this book. Thus, the oral optimistic constellation correlated significantly and positively with extraversion. The oral optimist is a stable extravert. The oral pessimist on the other hand is anxious. Thus these two syndromes essentially describe the extraverted and the anxious individual. The relationship of the anal character to the big five was even more striking. In a study of the authoritarian personality (Kline and Cooper, 1984a) in which Ai3Q was factored together with the 16PF test and a number of other measures of authoritarian personality, a clear obsessional or authoritarian factor emerged. As was argued in Kline (1992a) this factor resembles the openness to experience and conscientiousness factors of the big five. Thus in the concept of the anal character, there seems little doubt that Freud described a mixture of two of these big five factors.

At this point in the argument a brief aside is in order concerning the authoritarian personality. It does appear, as has been shown in earlier chapters of this book, that it is an important personality syndrome, characterised by obeisance to superiors and tough-minded control of inferiors. Genetic studies of this variable could be valuable since it is possible that this factor can be observed in the hierarchical ordering of many mammalian groups. This might account for the prevalence of authoritarian attitudes in human societies and the difficulty of eliminating them despite their unpleasant consequences.

To return to Freudian theory descriptively, Freud's psychosexual personality theory does not seem wide of the mark, although as has been seen these syndromes are mixtures of factors and the claimed aetiology is woefully short of empirical evidence. However, psychosexual personality syndromes are a relatively minor aspect of Freud's notions of personality and the factor analytic findings in the field of temperament are not really germane to his theorising, with its stress on the unconscious determinants of behaviour.

As regards the pertinence of the dynamic factors, ergs and sentiments, to Freudian theory, it must be said that it is not supported by these findings. Thus if psychoanalysis had been correct, two factors would have been expected, sexuality and aggression (even Eros and Thanatos) or possibly, only one – sexuality. However, this is not the case and there appears to be a longer list of dynamic factors.

However, the factor analyses of strength of interests which resulted in three main factors: alpha, conscious id; beta, realised ego; and gamma, the conscience factor, suggest that strength of interest is determined by three components of which only one, beta, is directly rational. This provides some confirmation for the Freudian notion that interests are determined by both conscious and unconscious factors. These results support the Freudian views in principle rather than in detail. They also cast doubt on the face-valid simple inventory approach to the study of attitudes and interests, a method which is concerned solely with the beta factor.

Other psychoanalytic theories

I do not want to discuss in any detail the pertinence of these factor analytic findings to other psychoanalytic theories because their influence in modern psychology is small. However, there are two points of interest.

First, Jung (1949) developed a typology of personality in which extraversion was an important category. Individuals were either extraverts or introverts and there were four categories of each. However, although extraversion is one of the main personality factors in the factor analytic conception, extraversion is a continuum and individuals may be placed anywhere on it. Jung's notion of an extraverted type is not supported by the evidence concerning the distributions of scores on tests, although these are of course dependent on the particular sets of items. Furthermore there has been no clear support for the eight fold categorisation, despite the popularity of the Myers–Briggs Type Indicator (Briggs and Myers, 1962).

Second, Adler (e.g. 1927) claimed that the basic drive for man was the upward striving for superiority to overcome feelings of inferiority and that most human behaviour could be understood in this way. This of course implies that there should be one large general motivational factor which is not the case. Adler however did stress the importance of within family differences affecting personality, notably family position, and this is supported by the genetic studies of the factors, discussed in Chapter 7.

Some other more recent theorists such as McClelland (1961) have argued a similar case regarding need achievement as a paramount drive. Again this is not supported by the factor analytic evidence which sees this variable as a composite of factors, self-assertion, career and self-sentiment being the most salient.

Conclusions In general these factorial findings give little support for psychoanalytic theories of personality which, in the main, do not deal with factors which have emerged as the most important, accounting for the most variance.

The work of Murray (1938) and McDougall (1932)

These are two of the most influential older theorists of personality and motivation and the work of Murray continues to spawn new tests (see those of Jackson, discussed in Chapter 5). McDougall (1932) argued that propensities were the basic drives, common to both mammals and human beings. However, most human activities are driven indirectly by sentiments. As is clear from this account, Cattell's motivational system is highly similar, in that he sees activities as resulting from the action of ergs and sentiments. Cattell, indeed, attempted to give McDougall's work an empirical, factor analytic basis.

Among McDougall's propensities were: food-seeking, disgust, sex, fear, protection, gregariousness, self-assertion, submission, anger, appeal, constructiveness, acquisition, laughter, comfort, sleep, migration, plus a number of bodily needs. From this list it appears that there is overlap with the ergs of Cattell, although McDougall claims more ergs than Cattell has replicated. Although there is some agreement with the hypothesised ergs, it must be remembered that Cattell's approach was influenced by McDougall's work.

As regards sentiments, there is no doubt that here McDougall proposed a far greater number than has been isolated by Cattell but his emphasis on the importance of the self-sentiment does receive support from factor analysis. In brief, there is surprisingly good support for this work from factor analysis although McDougall probably considerably overestimated the numbers of drives and sentiments.

As regards the work of Murray (1938), factor analysis is not supportive. He postulated on the basis of his personological studies which involved the most intensive research of individuals as whole people – hence the name – a long list of needs, few of which have been isolated by factor analysis. This is probably because Murray's needs were surface traits, close to observation, rather than the more fundamental source traits of factor analysis. Furthermore the tests which are based upon his needs, of which the best example is the PRF by Jackson (1974), technically an excellent test, have not been validated as a measure of needs. Indeed, as has been argued, there is evidence that the PRF is rather a measure of the big five (Costa and McCrae, 1988).

Situationalism

Mischel (1968) originally argued that the measurement of traits was not useful because in general correlations between traits and other criteria were low, around 0.3, on account of the fact that there was less consistency in behaviour than was assumed by the trait model, of which the psychometric model is a precise form. This was because, it was argued, there was so much variation in behaviour from situation to situation. This of course is perfectly true. Thus people shout at football matches and are quiet at funerals. In these original formulations, Mischel had used the fact of situational variation to argue that the notion of traits was not valuable and that trait measurement, the core of the psychometric view, was essentially worthless. In more recent publications (Mischel, 1984, for example), he has taken a less extreme line and stressed that in understanding behaviour the situation must be taken into account, but has admitted that personality traits are also influential.

As was mentioned above, it is perfectly obvious that situations affect behaviour. Furthermore, it is clear that situations interact with traits. Thus individuals high on anxiety are far more likely to be upset, if trapped in a cave, than those low on the variable, to take a simple example. However, there are interactions which are less immediately obvious. Thus individuals high on conscientiousness, one of the big five factors, react differently from those low on the factor when put in situations where conscientiousness is important – perhaps in vigilance tasks, such as examination marking. I do not refer here simply to conscientiousness at the task, but at anxiety over the accuracy of the scoring and the fairness of the procedure and so on.

Furthermore, it is apparent that over the long term there is real consistency in behaviour. To take well-known political examples, Mrs Thatcher was rarely submissive and Hitler was not ever tender-minded. To those critics of these claims who argue that this is due to stereotyping (Shweder, 1975), ask the relatives of the 6,000,000 who died in the concentration camps. In addition the work of Block (1971) shows considerable consistency in personality over time.

It should also be pointed out that many such political and social views and values have a considerable genetic determination, as was shown in some of the studies discussed in Chapter 7, notably Eaves *et al.* (1989).

Finally, of course, if personality traits were of no importance in understanding behaviour, the correlations with educational, occupational and clinical criteria, discussed in the last chapter, and the considerable hereditary, determination of the largest personality factors (see Chapter 7), would be inexplicable. What is required in any adequate psychometric view of personality is that situations be quantified and inserted into the relevant specification equations along with the ability, personality and motivational trait scores. This is a difficult project and one that psychometry has only just begun, although Cattell (1981) has outlined some possible but highly complex procedures.

Attribution theory

In our discussion of situationalism one of the arguments utilised by situationalists to account for the apparent consistency of individuals in everyday life was the notion of stereotyping, namely that people expect certain individuals to behave in certain ways. It is these expectations which create the consistency which is thus not real, in the sense of being part of the individual, but is an attribution of the observer. How an individual is cast, as it were, in her mould, depends on further stereotypes of appearance, national group, age, sex and the situations in which that individual is seen. As Eiser (1980) argues, attribution theory treats trait descriptions as a possible output from, rather than a possible input to, the process of person perception.

There is no doubt that judgements concerning personality traits are influenced by many of the cognitive and social factors discussed in attribution theory. Furthermore it is perfectly reasonable for social psychologists to elucidate the determinants of such judgements. It should be noticed, however, that the personality traits of psychometrics are not social judgements but factored test scores. Nevertheless that such social processes occur does not affect the status of traits as important determinants of personality.

Let me give an example from animal behaviour. It makes good sense to describe a cheetah as speedy. The fact that people so judge it to be on account of its muscular frame, its long legs and the reputation big cats have for speed, is irrelevant as to whether or not a cheetah is fast. This is capable of objective measurement. So it is with personality traits. Jews may be judged as mean or Blacks as lazy, but objective measures of these traits can ascertain whether such stereotypes are true or false.

As has been shown in our chapters on personality measurement, certain personality traits can be measured highly reliably and with good validity as judged by correlations with external criteria. Furthermore if traits were no more than explanatory fictions, their correlations with occupational and educational success and their high heritability ratios would make no sense. Thus attribution theory, interesting as it may be to social psychology, does not impugn the psychological importance of personality traits and thus the psychometric view of personality.

It is quite clear, from the discussion in this chapter, that none of the important theories of personality which have been scrutinised are supported by the psychometric results. In addition, there is one overarching criticism which applies to all of them and, indeed, to almost all the personality theories discussed in textbooks of personality, as Eysenck (1990) has argued. This concerns the results of the biometric analyses of personality where it was shown that between family differences did not contribute to variations in personality test scores (only two studies running against this trend). This is not only contra-intuitive but contrary to previous theories.

This means that it is necessary for psychometrics to develop its own theoretical account of the findings. There have been two outstanding attempts to do this by Eysenck (1967; Eysenck and Eysenck, 1976) and by Cattell (Cattell and Kline, 1977; Cattell, 1981), and these will now be described and evaluated. Both these writers have the most enormous outputs – Eysenck has more than 1,000 publications and Cattell in the region of 500, many long and technically formidable books. The references cited are the main sources of the theories but in a chapter of this length complete citation is difficult.

The work of Eysenck

To explicate the theory of Eysenck, I shall discuss the biological basis of the personality factors as claimed by Eysenck (1967), which was briefly mentioned in Chapter 4, and then discuss how these are related to conditioning and learning which are fundamental to understanding human behaviour, at least in Eysenck's view. I shall also discuss briefly how these theoretical views impinge on other important aspects of behaviour, such as neurosis and crime. Indeed, one of the most impressive features of Eysenckian personality theory is its applicability to real life as distinct from the psychological laboratory, although it is claimed also to be salient there.

Physiological factors In Eysenckian theory, extraversion is related to differences in cortical arousal (reticular formation activity) while neuroticism (or emotionality) has its basis in the limbic system, reflected in lability of the autonomic nervous system. Psychoticism appears to be related to differences in androgen level and other hormonal secretions which are themselves related to maleness.

However, as Claridge (1986) has well argued there are a number of problems with this physiological account which have led other leading workers in the field (e.g. Gray, 1982) to formulate a somewhat different story. Gray's physiological account, which is firmly rooted in physiology, although one based on rats rather than people, collapses neuroticism and introversion into a continuum of anxiety which, to quote Claridge, resembles a forty-five degree rotation of Eysenck's two factors, anxiety running diagonally from neurotic introversion to stable extraversion. However, Gray's system runs into difficulty with regard to P which he cannot accurately place in factor space.

The difficulty with the strict Eysenckian physiology lies in its complete separation of central nervous system arousal and autonomic activation. These, in reality, are unlikely to be entirely independent. This is what Gray (1982) has sought to correct by incorporating both into a single dynamic system.

Although there are problems with the physiological basis for these three factors, there is some agreement that these physiological systems are in some way involved. For example, despite the confusion of different findings, arousal as indicated by the EEG is related to introversion–extraversion (Gale and Eysenck, 1992). Some further support for this general physiological approach comes from two sources. Since the mammalian nervous system is highly similar to that of human beings, there should be some evidence of similar personality dimensions among mammals. Eysenck (1976) argues that this is indeed the case. Thus Broadhurst (1975) has studied emotionality in rats, a factor defined by faecal counts, and Chamove *et al.* (1972) have claimed to have identified all three factors in observations of rhesus monkeys.

If these factors are so intimately involved with such basic physiological differences, then the heritability ratios for the factors should be high. As has been fully discussed in Chapter 7 this is indeed the case, and even more interestingly, between family environmental differences do not seem to influence personality.

I shall not discuss the physiological basis of the Eysenckian factors further. This is sufficient to indicate that Eysenck has attempted to root these personality differences in biology, as is necessary for any adequate theory of personality.

Relation of E and N to conditioning and learning Eysenck (1967) treats N as a drive in the tradition of Hullian learning theory. Although he admits that not all studies are in agreement and that there are some anomalous results, he argues, as follows:

1 Emotion does act as a drive.
2 N refers to a dimension of greater emotional arousability.
3 High emotionality produces high drive in emotive situations.
4 Emotions acting as drives can hinder or facilitate performance depending on a number of interacting factors, including drive strength, task difficulty, experience and other personality factors, all of which should be included in any proper predictive equation.

There is one aspect of this formulation which does not seem to fit well with the factor analytic evidence discussed earlier in this book. In the studies of dynamic factor, anxiety or neuroticism did not appear as a drive.

It certainly affects learning but this may be as a temperamental rather than a drive factor.

In this approach to learning theory, reinforcement is seen as drive reduction, again in the Hullian tradition. However, drive reduction is limited to reduction of N, which is seen as a reaction to threat. Thus whatever reduces threat is reinforcing. This, as will be seen, is important in the Eysenckian conception of neurosis and its treatment.

As regards extraversion, Eysenck integrates this factor into learning, thus invoking excitation, which refers to cortical processes which facilitate learning, conditioning, memory, perception and mental processing in general, and the opposite of excitation inhibition, including satiation. This is, essentially, a statement of the psychophysiological underpinning of extraversion which was discussed in the previous section of this chapter.

From this Eysenck argued (1967) that introverts can be expected to condition more quickly and that their responses would be more resistant to extinction than extraverts, and that these differences would be greatest when the experimental conditions were such that the build-up of inhibition was maximised. When this last condition was met, Eysenck (1967) argued these predictions were supported although this qualification conveniently eliminates results which do not fit the findings.

However, there is a severe objection to this theorising of a link between conditioning and extraversion which was first made by Vernon (1963), namely that for it to be confirmed it would be necessary to show that conditionability was a unitary factor, i.e. that the same variables affected in the same way all conditioned responses. This is important because the experimental evidence applies only to three responses – eyeblink conditioning, GSR and verbal conditioning.

In the previous chapter it was seen that extraversion was related significantly and negatively to academic success (clearly a form of learning) although correlations are generally modest. However, the results from laboratory studies of the relation between extraversion and learning, as Eysenck (1967) admits, are difficult to summarise, except to say that there is some sort of significant relationship which might support the link between poor learning and cortical inhibition. However, to be more precise is difficult because there is so much variation depending upon experimental conditions. Certainly it would seem dubious, in the extreme, to extrapolate from these findings to real-life learning.

One feature of much of these results which does seem to be supported in occupational psychology, for example, as has been argued by Smith (1989), is that introverts are better at long and boring tasks, which tend to produce inhibition, while extraverts are better at brief and varied work.

Extraverts start better than introverts but, as inhibition builds up, begin to deteriorate and make errors, although they may pick up again towards the end. Extraverts are stimulus hungry and crave excitement, while introverts prefer the opposite.

This brief discussion of how learning is woven into his psychometric theory of personality indicates a number of severe difficulties with this aspect of Eysenck's theorising. First it is clear that, although Eysenck can explain them away, many results do not fit the theoretical predictions. Secondly, as Claridge (1986) has argued, there are some internal difficulties. Thus although arousal and activation are treated as separate properties (of the CNS and the ANS), at times they are linked together, one of the reasons that Gray (1982) attempted to modify physiological theories underpinning these factors. In addition, as has been argued, until conditionability has been shown to be unitary, the generalisability of the findings, even if they are accepted, is dubious.

One of the strengths of Eysenck's theory (although not an intrinsic part of it) is that it can be applied easily to real life behaviour, an extrapolation which Eysenck has not been loath to execute, despite the cautions which have been shown to be necessary.

As is well known, Eysenck has applied these theories to the analysis of psychotherapy and has attempted to develop a tight scientific rationale for behaviour therapy, based on classical conditioning theory. Classical conditioning is seen as the basis for the development of neurotic symptoms, as Eysenck (1982) argues. Cognitive concepts can be explained away in these terms by suitable operational definitions. Thus introverts who condition easily are likely to develop neurotic disturbances which are seen as conditioned emotional responses to be extinguished in behaviour therapy. However, as Lazarus (1986) has argued, such theorising is far too simplified and simplistic for clinical use.

In his studies of smoking Eysenck (1980) has implicated his personality factors in its determination and in the aetiology of disease, thus throwing doubt on the simple linkage between lung cancer and cigarette smoking. Similarly these factors have been implicated in sexual and marital satisfaction (Eysenck, 1976) and in criminality (Eysenck, 1977; Eysenck and Gudjonsson, 1989), although here there is the difficulty that criminality is not a unitary concept. Eysenck and Gudjonsson (1989) try to argue from the genetic influences which have been shown to be considerable for E, N and P (see Chapter 7) and the known relationships of these factors with criminality, that criminality might be expected to have similar hereditary determinants. This case is indeed supported by the greater concordance for criminal behaviour of MZ than DZ twins and by the fact that the criminality of adopted children is determined significantly by the criminality of their true parents. Indeed these authors show that estimates of heritability for criminality are about the same as for personality – in the region of 50–60 per cent. Again, this supports the influence of these psychometric personality traits on highly important aspects of social behaviour.

Conclusions It is clear from this discussion of Eysenck's theory of personality that it is one which has incorporated, as central elements, the factors which have emerged from his psychometric studies. His theory has a biological basis and is applicable to a wide range of behaviour. Nevertheless, despite its apparent elegance and clarity, all is not as simple as Eysenck would have us believe. There are too many experimental findings which do not fit the hypotheses and neurosis is not a simple matter of classical conditioning, just for example. However, as a basis for a theory open to development as new data are collected, this theory is excellent and it does what an adequate theory of personality must do – utilise the main factor analytic findings.

The work of Cattell

In the final section of this chapter I shall discuss the theoretical account of personality advocated by Cattell. This is undoubtedly the most complex, quantified, psychometric theory of personality which has ever been developed and it is derived from more than fifty years' continuous psychometry by Cattell and his colleagues.

The most comprehensive account of the theory is contained in the two volumes of Cattell (1981), a book of formidable mathematical complexity. A more simple description of the theory is to be found in Cattell and Kline (1977) and these are the best sources for an overall view of the theory, although certain aspects are dealt with in more detail in other individual publications, for example Cattell (1982) on the genetics of personality.

This summary account is derived from these sources in the main, together with Cattell (1985), but is necessarily stripped of detail, for in fact to describe the theory at all, huge numbers of researches and books have to be taken into consideration.

As has been discussed throughout this chapter the aim of a good psychometric theory of personality must be to make central the factors which have been discovered through factor analysis. For Eysenck this was a relatively straightforward procedure since his work is concerned with only three factors. For Cattell the position is entirely different. Thus, as has been seen in previous chapters, Cattell has developed the following sets of factors:

A Temperamental normal factors (measured by the 16PF and variants designed for different age groups).
B Abnormal factors (measured in the CAQ, but perhaps less central to a general theory of personality).
C Mood factors (measured by the Eight-State Questionnaire).
D Motivational Factors (measured by the CAT).
E Strength of interest factors (measured by the MAT).

All these factors and tests have been discussed in the relevant chapters of this book on temperament and dynamics.

F Ability factors. Actually, in addition to these personality factors, Cattell (e. g. 1971) has subjected the field of abilities to factor analysis and ability factors, which are beyond the purview of this book but are fully discussed in its companion volume *Intelligence: The Psychometric View* (Kline, 1991), form part of his theoretical structure.

Cattell is the doyen of psychometric personality theorists (and his approach and arguments inform this book). Thus his theory has been developed on the following principles:

1 Simple structure factor analyses are able, if the population of variables is properly sampled, to identify the most important variables. Thus the temperamental and dynamic factors which have been listed above must form the basis of any theory of personality.
2 Such factors must have reliable and valid tests. These, in Cattell's theory, are the tests listed above.
3 Psychometric personality theory has an underlying psychometric model, namely that a particular action of any individual can be defined by a specification equation which takes into account a subject's status on the five sets of factors discussed above, and the ambient situation, all of which are appropriately weighted for the particular act. If an action can be predicted or specified by a specification equation then it can be said to be understood. In this sense specification equations constitute theories of particular actions and the better the fit, the better the theory. As was discussed in Chapter 8, general specification equations for certain jobs and for certain clinical syndromes have been developed by Cattell and colleagues, using mainly the temperamental factors.
4 The development of all these factors needs to be studied so that factors determining personality can be understood. It is not sufficient to state,

in any theory, what the important factors are without specifying their aetiology. To this end Cattell has undertaken biometric studies (Cattell, 1982) discussed in Chapter 7 and has attempted further to specify determining features of the environment.

5 Cattell (1981) has developed a special learning theory, structured learning theory, which takes account of all these variables. This must be a part of any theory of human personality since, even though it is clear that there are important genetic components of variation, much of human behaviour is learned. This accepts the fact that learning involves multidimensional changes in the trait vector (the profile of scores on all factors), the bearing vector (which indicates the changing bearing of factors on performance, and an involvement vector (indicating the emotional involvement with the situation). Reinforcement, similarly, is defined as maximising tension reduction across all ergs, thus eliminating the circularity of the behaviouristic definition as that which increases the probability of response. This is not all, Cattell (1981) develops the econetic model which takes into account the stimulus, the situation, observer, personality and role, thus answering some of the objections from social psychology to the psychometric model.

6 It should be pointed out finally, that in this Cattellian theory, 'taken into account' does not mean some rather waffly discussion concerning the possible effects of observers on behaviour, for example. The econetic model and other yet more complex elaborations which Cattell (1982) specifies provide precise specification equations, although Cattell does admit that some of the mathematics is as yet speculative and requires new methods.

Discussion I shall not set out Cattell's theory in more detail than this, although in fact information about the tests and the variables, together with the factor analytic methods, are fully discussed in earlier chapters of this book. This is for two reasons. The first is that the principles of this theory, and its factor analytic methodology, seem to me to be the most important contribution to understanding personality from this work. Cattell's approach is precisely the one that a psychometric personality theorist should follow. However, as has been shown, there is some doubt about many aspects of the theory. Thus other workers have not been able to identify the factors as clearly as is necessary, if they are to form the props of a theory, and this is particularly true in the dynamic sphere. There is some doubt about the reliability and validity of the measuring devices. Finally, the algebra of the theorising of structured learning theory is so complex and not fully worked out that it is not possible to test it adequately. Indeed, it is possible that the linear algebra of this theory will have to be replaced by some less elegant but more applicable mathematical procedures.

Conclusions In brief, therefore, it is argued that this Cattellian theory constitutes a brilliant attempt to develop a proper psychometric theory of personality. It is a superb blueprint for other researchers and his contribution to the statistical methods, especially factor analysis, which are integral to such theorising, have been critically important and have been previously discussed. What needs to be done now, is to improve the identification of the factors and the psychometric statistical efficiency of the tests and to continue Cattell's pioneering work in building up specification equations, measuring situations and their interaction with factors, first efforts at which are mentioned in Cattell (1982), and in developing the new algebra necessary to accommodate the complexity of the equations. This is the task which awaits the psychometrics of personality.

Chapter 10

Summary and conclusions

In this chapter I shall summarise, as succinctly as possible, the main points in the psychometric view of personality.

1 The psychometric view of personality is an example of a trait theory.
2 Underlying the psychometric view of personality is the psychometric model of human behaviour.
3 The psychometric model is a specification equation in which any behaviour can be specified in terms of weighted scores on the main personality and ability factors.
4 It is the task of psychometric personality research to determine these specification equations, both the variables and the weights.
5 To this end personality tests are required. Examination of the three types – questionnaires or inventories, projective tests and objective tests – showed that only inventories and objective tests were suitable for the task.
6 Objective tests are not yet sufficiently developed to be useful for more than research and only factor analytic (because they are necessarily unitary) personality inventories can yield psychologically meaningful scores.
7 Factor analytic tests should be reliable and the factors need to be externally validated.
8 Simple structure oblique factor analyses have been shown to yield replicable and meaningful factors and the technical guidelines for producing such factors – adequate sampling of variables and subjects, the proper subject to variable ratio, choosing the correct number of factors and a rotational procedure which maximises the hyperplane count – are well established, as is the use of confirmatory analysis.
9 The factor analysis of temperamental personality tests has yielded five factors, the 'big five' – extraversion, neuroticism or anxiety, tough-mindedness, conscientiousness and open-mindedness.

10 The first three of these are well established, especially in the work of Eysenck and to a lesser extent Cattell, whose primary factors have proved difficult to replicate. The other two factors are possibly better subsumed as authoritarianism or obsessionality.
11 A study of other, temperamental personality inventories (not developed by factor analysis) revealed no new factors. Criterion-keyed tests, such as the MMPI, are useful only for screening.
12 Factoring in the abnormal sphere produced a number of factors of which the seven depression factors were of especial interest.
13 The study of dynamic factors has proved more difficult and there is less agreement about results. Strictly to ensure factors are dynamic, R analysis (of variables) is not satisfactory. Ideally P analysis (where the same individual's scores on many occasions are factored) is required. Short-term moods are difficult to capture.
14 As regards moods or states, it is possible that there are only two: negative and positive. However, subjects vary overall as to how moody they are.
15 Cattell has isolated seven strength of drive factors, of which three seem critical: alpha (conscious id), beta (realised ego) and gamma (morality). The significance of these factors is that in normal attitude scales, only beta is tapped. Thus they are unlikely to be valid.
16 With the same test (MAT) Cattell measures ten ergs and sentiments, ergs being basic biological drives and sentiments culturally-moulded drives. However, there is little agreement concerning these factors in a field which only Cattell has seriously investigated.
17 It is all these factors, together with ability factors which are beyond the scope of this book, which must be the elements in the psychometric view of personality and in the specification equations.
18 The heritability of three of the main personality factors, N, E and P, has been investigated and there are substantial genetic contributions to the population variance. Contrary to expectation between family environmental variance is not influential. Similar findings have been made with the big five.
19 There are substantial correlations between occupational membership and success and the personality factors. Cattell indeed has attempted to supply actual specification equations.
20 These factors have also proved useful in the prediction of educational attainment and in clinical diagnosis. They could be valuable also in the study of therapeutic treatment.
21 All these applied findings support the validity of the personality factors and the psychometric view of personality.
22 None of the well-known theories of personality adequately deals with

the personality variables shown to be salient by factor analysis. Thus these factor analytic studies impugn their validity. Furthermore their postulation of the importance of environmental factors in the development of personality is probably wrong and certainly exaggerated. Unique environmental experiences contribute to the environmental variance

23 Eysenck has developed a psychometric theory of personality which links his three factors to arousal, inhibition and activation in the nervous system and hence to conditioning. This theory has wide application to neurosis, crime and marital adjustment, just for example.

24 Problems with the unitary nature of conditionability and the fit of the theory to observations, especially in the sphere of clinical psychology, have prevented its wide acceptance.

25 Cattell has developed an even more comprehensive and elaborate theory of human behaviour which involves all his factors, including ability factors. Utilising structured learning theory and the econetic model he has attempted to draw up specification equations, even including situations. However, the algebraic complexity and the problems over the identification of factors and the reliability of his tests, renders the theory more of a brilliant blueprint than a substantive contribution.

26 However, it is clear that by the better identification of factors in both the temperamental and dynamic spheres and the elaboration of the measurement of situations, a powerful psychometric view of personality, in the form of specification equations (not necessarily linear) for a wide range of behaviours, can be drawn up.

References

Adler, A. (1927) *Understanding Human Nature*. New York, Chilton.

Adorno, T.W., Frenkel-Brunswick, E., Levinson, D.J. and Sandford, R.N. (1950) *The Authoritarian Personality*. New York, Harper & Row.

Allport, G.W. (1937) *Personality: A Psychological Interpretation*. New York, Holt, Rinehart & Winston.

Altmeyer, B. (1981) *Right-Wing Authoritarianism*. Winnipeg, University of Manitoba Press.

Amelang, M. and Borkenau, P. (1982) On the factor structure and external validity of some questionnaire scales measuring dimensions of extraversion and neuroticism (trans.) *Zeitschrift fur Differentiale Diagnostiche Psychologie*, 3, 119–146.

Arrindel, W.A. and van der Ende, J. (1985) An empirical test of the utility of the observation-to-variables ratio in factor and components analysis. *Applied Psychological Measurement*, 9, 165–178.

Ashkanasy, N.M. (1985) Rotter's internal–external scale. Confirmatory factor analysis and correlations with social desirability for alternative scale formats. Cited in Robinson, *et al.* (1991).

Bandura, A. and Walters, R.H. (1963) *Social Learning and Personality Development*. New York, Holt, Rinehart & Winston.

Barrett, P. and Kline, P. (1981) The observation-to-variable ratio in factor analysis. *Personality and Group Behaviour*, 1, 23–33.

Barrett, P. and Kline, P. (1982) Factor extraction: an examination of three methods. *Personality and Group Behaviour*, 2, 94–98.

Barton, K. and Cattell, R.B. (1981) *The Central State-Trait Kit (CTS): Experimental Version*. Champaign, Institute for Ability and Personality Testing.

Beck, A.T. (1962) Reliability of psychiatric diagnoses: a critique of systematic studies. *American Journal of Psychiatry*, 119, 210–215.

Bendig, A.W. (1959) Score reliability of dichotomous and trichotomous item responses in the MPI. *Journal of Consulting Psychology*, 23, 181–185.

Block, J. (1971) *Lives Through Time*. Berkeley, CA, Bancroft Books.

Blum, G.S. (1949) A study of the psychoanalytic theory of psychosexual development. *Genetic Psychology Monographs*, 39, 3–99.

Bolton, B.F. (1986) Clinical diagnosis and psychotherapeutic monitoring. 348–376 in Cattell, R.B. and Johnson, R.C. (eds) (1986).

Boyle, G.J. (1989) Re-examination of the personality type factors in the Cattell,

Comrey and Eysenck scales: were the factor solutions by Noller *et al.* optimal? *Personality and Individual Differences*, 10, 1289–1299.

Briggs, K.C. and Myers, I.B. (1962) *The Myers–Briggs Type Indicator.* Princeton, Educational Testing Service.

Broadhurst, P.L. (1975) The Maudsley reactive and non-reactive strains of rats – a survey. *Behavioural Genetics*, 5, 299–319.

Brown, R. (1965) *Social Psychology*. New York, Free Press.

Bryan, E. (1992) *Twins and Higher Multiple Births. A Guide to their Nature and Nurture.* Sevenoaks, Edward Arnold.

Buck, J.N. (1970) *The House Tree Person Technique: Revised Manual.* Los Angeles, West Psychological Services.

Buros, O.K. (ed.) (1979) *Eighth Mental Measurement Yearbook.* Highland Park, Gryphon Press.

Butcher, J.N. (1990) *MMPI–2 in Psychological Treatment.* New York, Oxford University Press.

Carroll, J.B. (1983) Individual differences in cognitive abilities. 213–235 in Irvine, S.H. & Berry, J.W. (eds) (1983).

Carstairs, G.S. (1957) *The Twice-Born: A Study of a Community of High Caste Hindus.* London, Hogarth Press.

Cattell, H. (1986) Clinical assessment by the 16PF, CAQ and MAT. 377–424 in Cattell, R.B. & Johnson, R.C. (eds) (1986).

Cattell, R.B. (1957) *Personality Motivation Structure and Measurement.* Yonkers, World Book Co.

Cattell, R.B. (1966) The Scree test for the number of factors. *Multivariate Behaviour Research*, 1, 140–161.

Cattell, R.B. (1971) *Abilities: their Structure Growth and Action.* New York, Houghton Mifflin.

Cattell, R.B. (1973) *Personality and Mood by Questionnaire.* San Francisco, Jossey-Bass.

Cattell, R.B. (1978) *The Scientific Use of Factor Analysis.* New York, Plenum.

Cattell, R.B. (1981) *Personality and Learning Theory*. New York, Springer.

Cattell, R.B. (1982) *The Inheritance of Personality and Ability.* London, Academic Press.

Cattell, R.B. (1985) *Human Motivation and the Dynamic Calculus.* New York, Praeger.

Cattell, R.B. and Bolton, L.S. (1969) What pathological dimensions lie beyond the normal dimensions of the 16PF? A comparison of MMPI and 16PF factor domains. *Journal of Consulting and Clinical Psychology*, 33, 18–29.

Cattell, R.B. and Butcher, H.J. (1968) *The Prediction of Achievement and Creativity.* New York, Bobbs Merrill.

Cattell, R.B. and Child, D. (1975) *Motivation and Dynamic Structure.* London, Holt, Rinehart & Winston.

Cattell, R.B., Eber, H.W. and Tatsuoka, M.M. (1970) *The 16 Factor Personality Questionnaire.* Champaign, Institute for Ability and Personality Testing.

Cattell, R.B. and Gibbons, B.D. (1968) Personality structure of the combined Guilford and Cattell Personality Questionnaires. *Journal of Personality and Social Psychology*, 9, 107–120.

Cattell, R.B., Horn, J.L. and Sweney, A.B. (1970) *Motivation Analysis Test.* Champaign, Institute for Ability and Personality Testing.

Cattell, R.B. and Johnson, R.C. (eds) (1986) *Functional Psychological Testing*. New York, Brunner Mazel.

Cattell, R.B. and Kline, P. (1977) *The Scientific Analysis of Personality and Motivation*. London, Academic Press.

Cattell, R.B. and Schuerger, J. (1976) *The O-A (Objective Analytic) Test Battery*. Champaign, Institute for Ability and Personality Testing.

Cattell, R.B. and Warburton, F.W. (1967) *Objective Personality and Motivation Tests*. Champaign, University of Illinois Press.

Chamove, A.S., Eysenck, H.J. and Harlow, H.F. (1972) Personality in monkeys: factor analysis of Rhesus social behaviour. *Quarterly Journal of Experimental Psychology*, 24, 496–504.

Child, D. (1991) *The Essentials of Factor Analysis* (second edition). London, Holt, Rinehart & Winston.

Christie, R. (1991) Authoritarianism and related constructs. 501–571 in Robinson, J.P. *et al.* (eds) (1991).

Claridge, G. (1985) *Origins of Mental Illness*. Oxford, Blackwell.

Claridge, G.S. (1986) Eysenck's contribution to the psychology of personality. 73–85 in Modgil, S. and Modgil, C. (eds) (1986).

Comrey, A.L. (1970) *The Comrey Personality Scales*. San Diego, Educational and Industrial Testing Service.

Cook, M. (1988) *Personnel Selection and Productivity*. Chichester, Wiley.

Cooper, C. and Kline, P. (1982) The internal structure of the Motivational Analysis Test. *British Journal of Educational Psychology*, 52, 228–233.

Cooper, C. and McConnille, C. (1989) The factorial equivalence of the state-extraversion positive affect and the state-anxiety negative affect. *Personality and Individual Differences*, 10, 919–920.

Cooper, C. and McConnille, C. (1990) Interpreting mood scores: clinical implications of individual differences in mood variability. *British Journal of Medical Psychology*, 63, 215–225.

Corah, N.L., Feldman, M.J., Cohen, I.S., Green, W., Meadow, A. and Rugwall, E.A. (1958) Social desirability as a variable in the Edwards Personal Preference schedule. *Journal of Consulting Psychology*, 22, 70–72.

Costa, P.T., Busch, C.M., Zondeman, A.B., Williams, R.B. and McCrae, R.R. (1986) Correlations of MMPI factor scales with measures of the five factor model of personality. *Journal of Personality Assessment*, 50, 640–650.

Costa, P.T. and McCrae, R.R. (1988) From catalogue to classification: Murray's needs and the five factor model. *Journal of Personality and Social Psychology*, 55, 258–265.

Costa, P.T. and McCrae, R.R. (in press). The Neo Personality Inventory (NEO-PI). In Briggs, S.R. and Cheek, J. (eds) (in press). *Personality Measures* (Vol. 1). Greenwich, JAI Press.

Costa, P.T., McCrae, R.R. and Holland, J.L. (1984) Personality and vocational interests in adulthood. *Journal of Applied Psychology*, 69, 390–400.

Costa, P.T., Zondeman, A.B., Williams, R.B. and McCrae, R.R. (1985) Content and comprehensiveness in the MMPI: an item factor analysis in a normal adult sample. *Journal of Personality and Social Psychology*, 48, 925–933.

Cronbach, L.J. (1951) Coefficient alpha and the internal structure of tests. *Psychometrika*, 16, 297–334.

Cronbach, L.J. (1976) *Essentials of Psychological Testing*. New York, Harper & Row.

Cronbach, L.J. (1984) *Essentials of Psychological Testing* (revised edition). New York, Harper & Row.

Cronbach, L.J. and Meehl, P.E. (1955) Construct validity in psychological tests. *Psychological Bulletin*, 52, 177–194.

Curran, J.B. and Cattell, R.B. (1974) *The Eight-State Questionnaire*. Champaign, Institute for Ability and Personality Testing.

Dahlstrom, W.G. and Walsh, G.S. (1960) *An MMPI Handbook*. London, Oxford University Press.

Darlington, C.P. (1970) *Heredity*, 25, 655–656.

Digman, J.N. (1990) Personality structure: emergence of the five factor model. *Annual Review of Psychology*, 41, 417–440.

Eaves, L.W., Martin, N.G. and Evsenck, H.J. (1989) *Genes Culture and Personality*. London, Academic Press.

Edwards, A.L. (1969) *Edwards Personal Preference Schedule*. New York, Psychological Corporation.

Eiser, J.R. (1980) *Cognitive Social Psychology*. London, McGraw-Hill.

Exner, J.E. (1986) *The Rorschach: A Comprehensive System* (second edition). New York, Wiley.

Eysenck, H.J. (1959) The Rorschach, in Buros, O.K. (ed.) (1959) *Fifth Mental Measurement Yearbook*, Highland Park, Gryphon Press.

Eysenck, H.J. (1967) *The Biological Basis of Personality*. Springfield, C.C. Thomas.

Eysenck, H.J. (1976) *Sex and Personality*. London, Open Books.

Eysenck, H.J. (1977) *Crime and Personality*. London, Routledge & Kegan Paul.

Eysenck, H.J. (1980) *The Causes and Effects of Smoking*. London, Temple Smith.

Eysenck, H.J. (1982) Neobehaviouristic (S-R) theory. 205–276 in Wilson, G.T. & Franks, C.M. (eds) (1982) *Contemporary Behaviour Therapy*. New York, Guilford Press.

Eysenck, H.J. (1989) Preface. In Friedman, A.F. *et al.* (1989).

Eysenck, H.J. (1990) Genetic and environmental contributions to individual differences: the three major dimensions of personality. *Journal of Personality*, 58, 245–261.

Eysenck, H.J. (ed.) (1961) *Handbook of Abnormal Psychology*. New York, Basic Books.

Eysenck, H.J. (ed.) (1970) *Readings in Extraversion–Introversion*. London, Staples Press.

Eysenck, H.J. and Eysenck, S.B.G. (1975) *The Eysenck Personality Questionnaire*. Sevenoaks, Hodder & Stoughton.

Eysenck, H.J. and Eysenck, S.B.G. (1969) *Personality Structure and Measurement*. London, Routledge & Kegan Paul.

Eysenck, H.J. and Eysenck, S.B.G. (1976) *Psychoticism as a Dimension of Personality*. London, Hodder & Stoughton.

Eysenck, H.J., Eysenck, S.B.G. and Barrett, P. (1992) *The EPQR*. Sevenoaks, Hodder & Stoughton.

Eysenck, H.J. and Gudjonsson, G. (1989) *The Causes and Cures of Criminality*. New York, Plenum Press.

Feldman, M. and Lewontin, R. (1975) The heritability hang up. *Science*, 190, 1163–1168.

Fenichel, O. (1945) *The Psychoanalytic Theory of Neurosis*. New York, Norton.

Ferguson, G.A. (1949) On the theory of test development. *Psychometrika*, 14, 61–68.

Floderus-Myrhed, B., Pedersen, N. and Rasmuson, I. (1980) Assessment of heritability for personality based on a short form of the Eysenck Personality Inventory: A study of 12,898 twin pairs. *Behavioural Genetics*, 10, 153–162.

Fontana, D. (1981) *Psychology for Teachers*. Leicester, British Psychological Society.

Freud, S. (1905) Three essays on sexuality. 135–243 in vol. 7 of *The Standard Edition of the Complete Psychological works of Sigmund Freud. London, Tavistock Press and the Institute of Psychoanalysis.*

Freud, S. (1911) Psychoanalytic notes on an autobiographical account of a case of paranoia (dementia paranoides). Vol. 3, 11, in *Collected Psychological Works of Sigmund Freud*. London, Hogarth Press and Institute of Psychoanalysis.

Freud, S. (1933) New Introductory Lectures. Vol. 22 of *The Standard Edition of the Collected Psychological Works of Sigmund Freud*. London, Hogarth Press and the Institute of Psychoanalysis, 1966.

Freud, S. (1939) *An Outline of Psychoanalysis*. London, Hogarth Press and the Institute of Psychoanalyis.

Friedman, A.F., Webb, J.T. and Lewak, R. (1989) *Psychological Assessment with the MMPI*. Hillsdale, Erlbaum.

Fromm, E. (1965) *The Heart of Man: Its Genius for Good or Evil*. London, Routledge & Kegan Paul.

Fulker, D.W. (1979) Nature and nurture: heredity. Chapter 5 in Eysenck, H.J. *The Structure and Measurement of Intelligence*. New York, Springer-Verlag.

Gale, A. and Eysenck, M.W. (eds) (1992) *Handbook of Individual Differences: Biological Perspectives*. Chichester, Wiley.

Ghiselli, E.E. (1966) *The Validity of Occupational Aptitude Tests*. New York, Wiley.

Gillis, J.S. (1986) Classroom achievement and creativity. 447–465 in Cattell, R.B. & Johnson, R.C. (eds) (1986).

Goldberg, L.R. (1983) The magical number five, plus or minus two: some considerations on the dimensionality of personality descriptors. Research Paper, Gerontology Research Center, Baltimore.

Gorsuch, R.L. (1974) *Factor Analysis*. Philadelphia, Saunders.

Gorsuch, R.L. (1986) Measuring attitudes, interest, sentiments and values. 316–333 in Cattell, R.B. & Johnson, R.C. (eds) (1986).

Graham, J.R. (1990) *MMPI–2 Assessing Personality and Pathology*. New York, Oxford University Press.

Gray, J.A. (1982) *The Neuropsychology of Anxiety*. Oxford, Clarendon Press.

Gruenbaum, A. (1984) *The Foundations of Psychoanalysis. A Philosophical Critique*. Berkeley, University of California Press.

Grygier, T.G. (1975) *The Dynamic Personality Inventory*. Windsor, NFER.

Grygier, T.G. and Grygier, P. (1976) *Manual to the Dynamic Personality Inventory*. Windsor, NFER.

Guilford, J.P. (1958) *Psychometric Methods*. New York, McGraw-Hill.

Guilford, J.P. (1959) *Personality*. New York, McGraw-Hill.

Guilford, J.P. (1967) *Human Intelligence*. New York, McGraw-Hill.

Guilford, J.S., Zimmerman, W.S. & Guilford, J.P. (1976) *The Guilford–Zimmerman Temperament Survey Handbook*. San Diego, EDITS.

Guthrie, G.M., Jackson, D.M., Astilla, R. and Elwood, B. (1981) Personality measurement: do scales have different meanings in another culture? Kingston

(Ontario), paper at Nato Conference on Human Assessment and Cultural factors.

Hakstian, A.R. (1971) A comparative evaluation of several prominent methods of oblique factor transformations. *Psychometrika*, 36, 175–193.

Hall, C.S. and Lindzey, G. (1957) *Theories of Personality*. New York, Wiley.

Hampson, S. and Kline, P. (1977) Personality dimensions differentiating certain groups of abnormal offenders from non-offenders. *British Journal of Criminology*, 17, 310–331.

Harman, H.H. (1976) *Modern Factor Analysis*. Chicago, University of Chicago Press.

Hathaway, S.R. and McKinley, J.C. (1951) *The Minnesota Multiphasic Personality Inventory Manual (Revised)*. New York, Psychological Corporation.

Heim, A.W. (1975) *Psychological Testing*. London, Oxford University Press.

Helmes, E. (1989) Evaluating the internal structure of the Eysenck Personality Questionnaire – objective criteria. *Multivariate Behavioural Research*, 24, 353–364.

Herriot, P. (ed.) (1989) *Assessment and Selection in Organisations*. Chichester, Wiley.

Holland, J.P. (1985a) *The Holland Vocational Preference Inventory*. Odessa, Psychological Assessment Resources.

Holland, J.P. (1985b) *Making Career Choices: A Theory of Personality Types and Work Environments*. Englewood Cliffs, Prectice-Hall.

Holley, J.W. (1973) Rorschach analysis. 119–155 in Kline, P. (ed.) (1973).

Holtzman, W.H. (1981) Holtzman Inkblot Technique. 47–83 in Rabin, A.I. (ed.) (1981).

Horn, J. and Knapp, J.R. (1973) On the subjective character of the empirical base of Guilford's structure of intellect model. *Psychological Bulletin*, 80, 33–43.

Howarth, E. (1976) Were Cattell's personality sphere factors correctly identified in the first instance? *British Journal of Psychology*, 67, 213–230.

Howarth, E. (1980) *Technical Background and User Information for State and Trait Inventories*. Alberta, University of Alberta Press.

Hundleby, J.D. (1973) The measurement of personality by objective tests. 65–87 in Kline, P. (ed.) (1973).

Irvine, S.H. and Berry, J.W. (eds) (1983) *Human Assessment and Cultural Factors*. New York, Plenum.

Jackson, D.N. (1974) *The Personality Research Form*. New York, Research Psychologists Press.

Jennrich, C.I. and Sampson, P.F. (1966) Rotation for simple loadings. *Psychometrika*, 31, 313–323.

Jensen, A. (1980) *Bias in Mental Testing*. New York, Free Press.

Jewell, L.N. and Siegall, M. (1990) *Contemporary Industrial/Organisational Psychology*. New York, West Publishing Co.

Jinks, J.L. and Fulker, J.W. (1970) Comparison of the biometrical, genetical, MAVA and classical approaches to the study of human behaviour. *Psychological Bulletin*, 73, 311–349.

John, O.P. (1990) The big five factor taxonomy: dimensions of personality in natural language and in questionnaires. 66–100 in Pervin, L. (ed.) *Handbook of Personality Theory and Research*. New York, Guilford Press.

Johnson, J.R., Null, C., Butcher, J.N. and Johnson, K.N. (1984) Replicated item level factor analyses of the full MMPI. *Journal of Personality and Social Psychology*, 47, 105–114.

Joreskog, K.G. (1973) General methods for estimating a linear structural equation system. In Goldberger, A.S. & Duncan, A.D. (eds) (1973) *Structural Equation Models in the Social Sciences*. New York, Seminar Press.

Joreskog, K G. and Sorbom, D. (1979) *Advances in Factor Analysis and Structural Equation Models*. Cambridge, MA, Abt Books.

Jung, C.G. (1910) The association method. *American Journal of Psychology*, 21, 219–269.

Jung, C.G. (1940) *The Integration of the Personality*. London, Routledge & Kegan Paul.

Jung, C.G. (1949) *Psychological Types*. London, Routledge & Kegan Paul.

Kameoka, V.A. (1986) The structure of the Clinical Analysis Questionnaire and depression symptomatology. *Multivariate Behavioural Research*, 21, 105–121.

Kline, P. (1966) Extraversion, neuroticism and academic performance among Ghanaian university students. *British Journal of Educational Psychology*, 36, 93–94.

Kline, P. (1968) Obsessional traits, obsessional symptoms and anal erotism. *British Journal of Medical Psychology*, 49, 299–305.

Kline, P. (1971) *Ai3Q*. Windsor, National Foundation for Educational Research.

Kline, P. (1975) *The Psychology of Vocational Guidance*. London, Batsford.

Kline, P. (1979) *Psychometrics and Psychology*. London, Academic Press.

Kline, P. (1981) *Fact and Fantasy in Freudian Theory* (second edition). London, Methuen.

Kline, P (1986) *Handbook of Test Construction*. London, Routledge and Kegan Paul.

Kline, P. (1988) *Psychology Exposed: Or the Emperor's New Clothes*. London, Routledge.

Kline. P. (1991) *Intelligence: The Psychometric View*. London, Routledge.

Kline, P. (1992a) *The Handbook of Psychological Testing*. London, Routledge.

Kline, P. (1992b) *Psychometric Testing in Personnel Selection and Appraisal*. Kingston, Kroner.

Kline, P and Barrett, P. (1983) The factors in personality questionnaires among normal subjects. *Advances in Behaviour Research and Therapy*, 5, 141–202.

Kline, P. and Cooper, C. (1982) The internal structure of the Motivation Analysis Test. *British Journal of Educational Psychology*, 52, 228–233.

Kline, P. and Cooper, C. (1984a) A factorial analysis of the authoritarian personality. *British Journal of Psychology*, 75, 171–176.

Kline, P. and Cooper, C. (1984b) A construct validation of the Objective Analytic Test Battery (OATB). *Personality and Individual Differences*, 5, 328–337.

Kline, P. (ed.) (1973) *New Approaches in Psychological Measurement*. Chichester, Wiley.

Kline, P. and Grindley, J. (1974) A 28-day case study with the MAT. *Journal of Multivariate Experimental Personality and Clinical Psychology*, 1, 13–32.

Kline, P. and Lapham, S. (1990) *The PPQ*. Exeter, University of Exeter.

Kline, P. and Lapham, S. (1991) The validity of the PPQ: a study of its factor structure and its relation to the EPQ. *Personality and Individual Differences*, 12, 631–635.

Kline, P. and Storey, R. (1977) A factor analytic study of the oral character. *British Journal of Social and Clinical Psychology*, 166, 317–328.

Kline, P. and Storey, R. (1978) The Dynamic Personality Inventory: what does it measure? *British Journal of Psychology*, 69, 375–383.

Kohn, P.M. (1972) The authoritarian-rebellion scale: a balanced F scale with left-wing reversals. *Sociometry*, 35, 171–189.

Kreitler, S. and Kreitler, K. (1990) *The Cognitive Foundations of Personality Traits.* New York, Plenum.

Krug, S.E. (1980) *Clinical Analysis Questionnaire.* Champaign, Institute for Ability and Personality Testing.

Kuder, G.F. (1970a) *Kuder General Interest Survey.* Chicago, Science Research Associates.

Kuder, G.F. (1970b) *Kuder Occupational Interests Survey.* Chicago, Science Research Associates.

Lacan, J. (1966) *Ecrits.* Paris, Seuil.

Layton, C. (1985) The relationship between externality and E, N, P and L: an experiment and review. *Personality and Individual Differences,* 6, 505–507.

Lazarus, A.A. (1986) On sterile paradigms and the realities of clinical practice: critical comments on Eysenck's contribution to behaviour therapy. 247–257 in Modgil, S. & Modgil, C. (eds) (1986).

Lefcourt, H.M. (1991) Locus of control. 413–499 in Robinson, J.P. *et al.* (eds) (1991).

Likert, R.A. (1932) A technique for the measurement of attitudes. *Archives of Psychology,* 140.

Loehlin, J. (1992) *Genes and Environment in Personality Development.* Newbury Park, CA, Sage.

Loehlin, J.C. and Nichols, R.C. (1976) *Heredity, Environment and Personality: A Study of 850 Sets of Twins.* Austin, University of Texas Press.

Magnusson, D. and Endler, N.S. (eds) (1977) *Personality at the Crossroads: Current Issues in Interactional Psychology.* Hillsdale, Erlbaum.

Martin, N. and Jardine, R. (1986) Eysenck's contribution to behaviour genetics. 13–47 in Modgil, S. and Modgil, C. (eds) (1986).

McClelland, D.C. (1961) *Achieving Society.* Princeton, Van Nostrand.

McCormick, E.J., Jeanneret, P.R. and Mecham, R.C. (1972) A study of job characteristics and job dimensions as based on the Position Analysis Questionnaire (PAQ). *Journal of Applied Psychology,* 56, 347–368.

McCrae, R.R. and Costa, P.T. (1985) Comparison of EPI and psychoticism scales with measures of the five factor theory of personality. *Personality and Individual Differences,* 57, 17–40.

McCrae, R.R. and Costa, P.T. (1987) Validation of the five factor model of personality across instruments and observers. *Journal of Personality and Social Psychology,* 52, 81–90.

McCrae, R.R. and Costa, P.T. (1989a) Rotation to maximise the construct validity of factors in the NEO Personality Inventory. *Multivariate Behavioural Research,* 24, 107–124.

McCrae, R.R. and Costa, P.T. (1989b) Reinterpreting the Myers–Briggs Type Indicator from the perspective of the five factor model of personality. *Journal of Personality,* 57, 17–40.

McCrae, R.R, and Costa, P.T. (1990) *Personality in Adulthood.* New York, Guilford.

McCrae, R.R. and John, O.P. (in press) An introduction to the five-factor model of personality and its applications. *Journal of Personality* (in press).

McDougall, W. (1932) *Energies of Men.* London, Methuen.

Mischel, W. (1968) *Personality and Assessment.* New York, Wiley.

Mischel, W. (1977) The interaction of person and situation. In Magnusson, D. & Endler, N. S. (eds) (1977).

Mischel, W. (1984) *Introduction to Personality* (fourth edition). Tokyo, CBS.

Modgil, S. and Modgil, C. (eds) (1986) *Hans Eysenck: Consensus and Controversy*. London, The Falmer Press.

Murray, H.A. (1938) *Explorations in Personality*. Oxford, Oxford University Press.

Murstein, B.I. (1963) *Theory and Research in Projective Techniques*. New York, Wiley.

Nesselroade, J.R. and Baltes, P.B. (1975) Higher-order convergence of two distinct personality systems: Cattell's HSPQ and Jackson's PRF. *Multivariate Behaviour Research*, 10, 387–408.

Noller, P., Law, H. and Comrey, A.L. (1987) Cattell, Comrey and Eysenck personality factors compared: more evidence for the five robust factors. *Journal of Personality and Social Psychology*, 53, 775–782.

Norman, W.T. (1963) Towards an adequate taxonomy of personality attributes. *Journal of Abnormal and Social Psychology*, 65, 574–583.

Nunnally, J.O. (1978) *Psychometric Theory*. New York, McGraw-Hill.

Parker, C. and Kline, P. (1992) The psychological meaning of the VPI scales. *Personality and Individual Differences* (in press).

Pervin, L. (ed.) (1990) *Handbook of Personality Theory and Research*. New York, Guilford Press.

Phares, E.J. (1976) *Locus of Control in Personality*. Morristown, General Learning Press.

Phillipson, H. (1955) *Object Relations Technique*. London, Tavistock Publications.

Plomin, R. (1986) *Development, Genetics and Psychology*. Hillsdale, Erlbaum.

Popper, K. (1959) *The Logic of Scientific Discovery*. New York, Basic Books.

Rabin, A.I. (ed.) (1981) *Assessment with Projective Techniques*. New York, Springer.

Ray, J.J. (1970) The development and validation of a balanced dogmatism scale. *Australian Journal of Psychology*, 22, 253–260.

Robinson, J.P., Shaver, P.R. and Wrightsman, L.S. (eds) (1991) *Measures of Personality and Social Psychological Attitudes*. New York, Academic Press.

Rokeach, M. (1960) *The Open and Closed Mind*. New York, Basic Books.

Rorschach, H. (1921) *Psychodiagnostics*. Berne, Hans Huber.

Rose, R.J., Koskenvuo, M., Kaprio, J., Sarna, S. & Langinvainio, N. (1988) Shared genes, shared experiences, and similarity of personality. *Journal of Personality and Social Psychology*, 164–171.

Rotter, J.B. (1966) Generalised expectancies for internal vs. external control of reinforcement. *Psychological Monographs*, 80, No. 609.

Rotter, J.B. (1975) Some problems and misconceptions related to the construct of external versus internal control of reinforcement. *Journal of Consulting and Clinical Psychology*, 43, 56–67.

Royce, J.R. (1963) Factors as theoretical constructs. Chapter 24 in Jackson, D.N. & Messick, S. (eds) (1967) *Problems in Human Assessment*. New York, McGraw-Hill.

Semeonoff, B. (1977) *Projective Tests*. Chichester, Wiley.

Shields, J. (1962) *Monozygotic Twins*. Oxford, Oxford University Press.

Shweder, R.A. (1975) How relevant is an individual difference theory of personality? *Journal of Personality*, 43, 455–485.

Skinner, B.F. (1953) *Science and Human Behaviour*. New York, Macmillan.

Smith, M. (1989) Selection in high-risk and stressful occupations. 557–576 in Herriot, P. (ed.) (1989).

Stone, W.F. and Lederer, G. (eds) (1991) *Strength and Weakness: The Authoritarian Personality Today*. New York, Springer-Verlag.

Stricker, L.J. and Ross, R. (1964) An assessment of some structural properties of the Jungian Personality Typology. *Journal of Abnormal and Social Psychology*, 68, 62–71.

Strong, E.K. and Campbell, D.P. (1974) *Strong–Campbell Interest Inventory* (Revised edition). Stanford, Stanford University Press.

Strong, E.K., Campbell, D.P., Berdie, R.E. and Clerk, K.E. (1971) *Strong Vocational Interest Blank*. Stanford, Stanford University Press.

Sweney, A.B., Anton, M.T. and Cattell, R.B. (1986) Evaluating motivation structure, conflict and adjustment. 288–315 in Cattell, R.B. & Johnson, R.C. (eds) (1986).

Sweney, A.B. and Cattell, R.B. (1980) *The Vocational Interest Measure*. Champaign, Institute for Ability and Personality Testing.

Tellegen, A., Lykken, D.T., Bouchard, T.J., Wilcox, K., Segal, N. and Rich, S. (1988) Personality similarity in twins reared apart and twins reared together. *Journal of Personality and Social Psychology*, 54, 1031–1039.

Thurstone, L.L. (1947) *Multiple Factor Analysis: A Development and Expansion of Vectors of the Mind*. Chicago, University of Chicago Press.

Tupes, E.C. and Christal, R.E. (1961) Recurrent Personality factors based on Trait Ratings. *USAF ASD Technical Report*, Lackland, U.S. Air Force.

Velicer, W.F. (1976) Determining the number of components from the matrix of partial correlations. *Psychometrika*, 41, 321–327.

Vernon, P.E. (1950) *The Measurement of Abilities*. London, University of London Press.

Vernon, P.E. (1963) *Personality Assessment*. London, Methuen.

Vernon, P.E. (1964) *Personality Assessment*. London, Methuen.

Vetter, H.J. & Smith, B.D. (eds) (1971) *Personality Theory: A Source Book*. New York, Appleton-Century-Crofts.

Watson, D. & Tellegen, A. (1985) Towards a consensual structure of mood. *Psychological Bulletin*, 98, 219–235.

Name index

Subject index